I Didn't Want to Do It!

Memoir of a **Sinner** Turned **Megachurch Builder**

Donald Earl Bryant, DMin

Foreword by John W Waters, PhD

I Didn't Want to Do It!

For bulk quantity orders or for more information, contact the publisher:
Dr. Donald Earl Bryant
debryantbooks@gmail.com
P. O. Box 281
Madison, TN 37116

ISBN: 978-1-7362236-0-4

LIBRARY OF CONGRESS CONTROL NUMBER: 2021906799

Printed in the United States

Publishing Services Provided By Guardian Angel Communications Services
Nashville, Tennessee
gangelcs1997@gmail.com • (615) 228-2688

Dedication

I dedicate this memoir to my parents, the late Mr. James Bryant, Sr., and Mrs. Mamie King Bryant. My parents were indeed the bedrock of our family. Even during Alabama's brutal racial oppression and the inequities that were present across the spectrum of our existence, James and Mamie Bryant were able, by the grace of God, to stand firm and meet the challenges they faced. They maintained a strong family unit. I can never say enough about how they were able to endure, persevere, and model impeccable composure and character, as did other family members, along with other African-American members of the Dolomite community.

I am eternally grateful to God for giving us our parents!

Contents

Acknowledgments

I want to express deep appreciation and gratitude to the Friendship Community Church family for allowing me to serve as pastor and support the vision God gave me. Friendship took a leap of faith with me, believing that God had called and empowered me to lead their congregation. Although Friendship was my first and only pastorate, God made it possible for me to serve there for thirty-three years, twenty-eight of those years as pastor.

I talk about the people of Friendship Community Church everywhere I go. It is because of the members that Friendship can spread the love of God and resources beyond the four walls of the church building. They proved to be people willing to serve and bring the Kingdom of God to earth in real-time. They have allowed God to use them so that miracles happen, and the church continues to serve as a beacon within the community. Thank you, Friendship!

I would like to give special thanks to Deacon Henry Carter for his assistance in preparing this manuscript and Brenda Williams for standing ready to support and lead wherever she was asked to serve.

My family has always been incredibly unique to me. I am thankful for my brother, James Jr., who served as an inspiration for me during

Donald and Brenda Bryant

my formative years. I'm grateful for my sisters, Sandra and Beverly, who were always there for me; after all, I was the baby. Although not mentioned here by name, many other family members have had a tremendous impact on my life. They gave real meaning to the word "family." My aunts, uncles, and cousins always were able to carry out their responsibilities as family members.

I am thankful for my wife, Brenda, who trusted God and married me. Then God gave us a special gift—a one-pound, seven-ounce premature baby girl we named Rachel Michelle. Her name means, "Motherly, who is like the Lord." She made us enormously proud throughout her college pursuits at Alabama State University (ASU). Rachel earned a Bachelor of Arts degree in theatre from ASU and a Master of Fine Arts degree from Florida Atlantic University.

I'm deeply grateful for my grandchildren, Rebekah and Isaiah. As the songwriter penned, "God has been good to me!"

Donald Earl Bryant, DMin
Pastor Emeritus, Friendship Community Church

Foreword

My professional teaching career began in 1957 as a science and math teacher with the public school system of Atlanta. I discovered early on that there were two types of students who would make a lasting impression: the excellent student, and the poor student who often presented discipline problems. As I matured in the teaching profession, I began to distinguish myself as a professional educator and more than just a teacher. From early childhood on, my desire was to provide my students with a solid foundation to build on and become successful.

For me, the idea of success stated is: "Success is the continuous movement toward predetermined, worthwhile goals, with emphasis upon predetermined." This statement is not an original thought, but after several decades as a professional educator, I have seen many former students achieve much success in their lives—among these is Dr. Donald Earl Bryant.

In this foreword, we can refer to him as Dr. Bryant, Pastor Bryant, or Brother Bryant. Each term has come to mean a great deal to me.

"Equipping the saints for ministry" (Ephesians 4:12) is perhaps the briefest and most precise way to describe the ministry and legacy of Donald

Earl Bryant from Dolomite, Alabama. Equipping the saints is how I have seen him grow as a minister and developer of a church.

My relationship with Pastor Bryant began when he became a student at Morehouse School of Religion (MSR) at the Interdenominational Theological Seminary (ITC) in the mid-1980s. I was a professor of the Hebrew Bible (Old Testament), and he was enrolled in one of the introductory courses I taught. He took several Old Testament courses from me and proved to be a competent and attentive student.

Brother Bryant's and my relationship with the Friendship Baptist Church of College Park, Georgia, came through our relationship with the late Dr. Charles Jackson Sargent, Jr., then senior pastor of Friendship, administrative vice president of ITC, and a professor of homiletics there. Brother Bryant became the youth minister at Friendship while still a student at ITC.

Dr. Sargent later retired, and the church called Pastor Bryant. It was Pastor Bryant who moved the church from downtown College Park to unincorporated College Park. This memoir goes into detail about what happened in the process.

Under Pastor Bryant's leadership, the church relocated to a campus of almost seventy acres in South Fulton, Georgia. Friendship has some eighty ministries. The one that impressed me most is the Sitting Ministry for those who are not involved in other ministries, but visit and sit with the homebound so that their caregivers can have some relief.

The church was renamed Friendship Community Church, a reflection of Bryant's realization that if the congregation was to serve the community, the Baptist notation had to change.

Dr. Bryant and I were highly active in the New Era Missionary Baptist Convention of Georgia. Together we served on the nomination committee, the budget committee, and probably others.

One of the most lasting achievements that we accomplished was our involvement with the purchase and development of the New Era Missionary Baptist Convention Center in Griffin, Georgia. We were members of the

Council of Overseers, which I chaired. Under the council's leadership, the center acquired a site of approximately one hundred acres, making the center the largest Black-owned property in Spalding County, Georgia.

Pastor Bryant has been a continuous student since I have known him. Reading Paul's letters to Brother Timothy reminds me of how I have seen Brother Bryant's growth and development. Paul tells Timothy to study to show himself a workman, not ashamed. Often, this text is mistaken in referring only to learning the Bible; there is much more to it than this. Bryant knew the importance of a sound theological education. He did not stop his education with a business degree from Tuskegee or a Master of Divinity (MDiv) degree from ITC. He pursued and earned the Doctor of Ministry (DMin) degree, which gives him the rightful title of Dr. Donald Earl Bryant.

Dr. Bryant was concerned not only with his education, but he brought his love and commitment to education to Friendship Church. He established and personally financed a 529 Educational Scholarship Fund for each child at Friendship. High school graduates are presented with scholarships to pursue wherever careers they desire.

Pastor Bryant's love for children was most clear each First Sunday, when the church's youth were in full participation during the morning worship. The choir loft was filled with children, from the youngest to teenagers, singing and praising God. A youth ambassador would always give the opening invocation.

At this point, let me mention the teaching aspect of Dr. Bryant's ministry. The sermons were always a timely, uplifting, and intellectual challenge. They always ended on an affirmational note. Sometimes data would be given to support the primary focus of the message. There was always that essential spiritual component, to be clear, that the center of our lives should be living Jesus' commandments.

Previously, I mentioned the expansive church campus. I did not note, however, that under Bryant's administration, the church became and remains debt-free. The absence of debt speaks to the financial stability of the church. There is now in place an endowment that assures proper maintenance of the property. At Pastor Emeritus Bryant's retirement, he left a legacy that includes numerous employees, full-time staff, other ongoing activities—including a fully functional gym open to the community—and most importantly, the freedom of being debt-free.

Why would I take time to compose this foreword?

I have witnessed the development of a Christian ministry based on sound biblical and common-sense principles. My seminary teaching began at the School of Theology at Boston University more than fifty years ago.

Many of my former students have had successful careers in a variety of areas, but none did I come to call my pastor. I have seen Brother Bryant living out 1 Timothy 3:1–7. Bryant has lived out Paul's admonition to Timothy in 2 Timothy 4:1–8.

Dr. Donald Earl Bryant has demonstrated a strong personality with character. He has been faithful to his ordination and the church to which he received the call to serve. I have found him trustworthy and reliable, a person with high moral standards and values.

Over these many years, Brother Bryant has become a dear, dear friend, a confidant, and my pastor.

Reading Bryant's memoir should prove helpful to anyone interested in the life of the church. It demonstrates that out of struggle and conflict can come the strength to hold fast to personal standards. He built a megachurch congregation that, under his administration, is debt-free. Given the effort that so many non-profits have with funding, to understand how to move a somewhat diverse group to full cooperation, Bryant's approach could prove most beneficial. Bryant also lays out a process for pastoral transition, which can be extremely helpful.

To God be the glory for the work and ministry of Donald Earl Bryant, who has been in the world, reconciling it to God through Jesus Christ. The Kingdom work that Dr. Bryant has done speaks for him.

John W Waters, PhD
Atlanta, Georgia

Introduction

I Didn't Want to Do It

But Moses replied to the LORD, "Please, Lord, I have never been eloquent—either in the past or recently or since you have been speaking to your servant—because my mouth and my tongue are sluggish." The LORD said to him, "Who placed a mouth on humans? Who makes a person mute or deaf, seeing or blind? Is it not I, the LORD? Now go! I will help you speak and I will teach you what to say." Moses said, "Please, Lord, send someone else" Exodus 4:10–13 (CSB).

This book encourages people involved in ministry and doing work that they did not want to do. These reflections hopefully will inspire you regarding the power and effectiveness of God, even when your passion for the assignment is lacking.

Scripture is replete with examples of people who were called by God but were reluctant to heed that call. In serving, however, obedience to God's call always results in blessings beyond measure. That is why I cited Moses' work; he did not want to do what God was calling him to, but in the end, the Israelites received deliverance from four hundred years of slavery under the oppressive hand of the pharaohs.

This reflective work will show you how God can accomplish great things in your life, even if the obstacles you face seem impossible to overcome.

At the same time, hopefully my story demonstrates that it is not how inadequate you think you are; but rather, it is all about God!

Following God, even when you don't want to do it, will bless not only your life but also the lives of those with whom you associate. Looking back at my life, I now see firsthand what God was dealing with in me.

It is incredible how the Lord led us from a small church at 1971 West Harvard Avenue, College Park, Georgia, to a campus of sixty-six acres with 88,000 square feet of ministry space at 4141 Old Fairburn Road (in what was then unincorporated Fulton County and is now the City of South Fulton), debt-free! More importantly, thousands of people from every walk of life united with the church and actively participated in the ministries God provided for us.

And I did not want to do it! I had not charted a path for my life that included ministry.

It all started on April 9, 1950, Resurrection Sunday morning, when James Bryant, Sr., and Mamie King Bryant welcomed the latest addition to their loving, but economically poor family in Dolomite, Alabama. Donald Earl Bryant is the youngest of four children—brother: James, Jr., and sisters: Sandra Jean and Beverly Ann.

Our family lived in a two-room house facing Pleasant Grove Road, a paved thoroughfare. To our rear were other houses on dirt roads. Most people in this community were employed at steel and coal factories, making meager wages that supplied the necessities for living.

The houses we lived in were referred to as "company" houses because years earlier, the factory owners had built houses for workers, and over time, workers could buy them through payroll deductions. Others were able to build their own homes in the community of Dolomite.

All the people from Pleasant Grove Road eastward were African Americans, while on the other side of the street westward were White residents. To an observant onlooker, there were noticeable socioeconomic differences just 150 feet from our front door.

On the north side of our home was Dolomite Elementary School, which we attended first through sixth grades—all African-American students were taught by African Americans. About a half-mile south was another elementary school, attended by White children only.

Most African Americans in Dolomite did not have automobiles, televisions, or indoor bathroom facilities. During the winter, we used coal for heating and cooking, and in the summer, we fanned ourselves with pieces of cardboard to keep cool.

The people in the community raised hogs and chickens in their yards and planted vegetables for food. When our Uncle Jim Smith killed a hog, the activity was like a family reunion. All family members gathered and shared the cooked food and received portions of the hog to take home.

Throughout the community, people were very caring and shared their goods, much like the early church believers in Acts 4:32. Though impoverished, starvation was not a reality among Blacks in Dolomite. The people realized that they needed one another, and because of that, we were able to survive.

Andrew Lee Smith, my mother's elder sister, worked in the cafeteria at the elementary school for White children. Every day, our aunt "Tee Tee" as we called her, walked home from work with cornbread and other cafeteria leftovers.

I remember that cornbread being the best I'd ever had. Our aunt was among many people in our neighborhood who walked miles to work, as automobiles were rare. Rest breaks at work, too, were few for African-American workers.

Tee Tee was an excellent cook. We frequently ate entrées at her house. She did not serve familiar dishes like the ones we had at home every day or even on Sundays. Instead, she prepared some of the meals she'd cooked for White people. It was like eating in a fancy restaurant.

Within our poor but loving Black community, there were occasional small signs of progress. I vividly recall when, in 1958, the Epps family became the first to install an indoor toilet. It was the talk of Black

Dolomite! Ours was a tight-knit community, but our homes were distinctly different from those in the neighborhood directly across the street. The amenities they enjoyed because of their skin color were benefits we could not fathom for ourselves. For instance, there was no evidence of outdoor toilets behind the houses owned and occupied by Whites. And it seemed that in every driveway of every house in their neighborhood, there was an automobile.

At the time, the reason why White people lived "better" was not a question in my young mind, although I'm sure African-American adults pondered the issue all the time. Although we were economically challenged, our financial status was neither a focus nor a consideration for our neighborhood children. We learned to enjoy what little we had. The adults were not able to buy toys for their children; however, the elders taught us how to build our toys, which also challenged our creativity. Discarded push wagons with wheels collected from dumps, race cars, slingshots, bow and arrows, skateboards, and playhouses were among the gifts that children in the community learned how to make by hand.

Mr. Ossie Walton, who did not own a truck or an automobile, was the housebuilder in the community. He carried his tools with him, using only a hammer, a hand saw, and nails to build a complete house from the ground up.

Mr. Willie Epps cut men's hair in an enclosed rear section of his home, while Mr. Flowers walked throughout the community, cutting men's hair. Mrs. Florence Black had a beauty salon inside her home, while Mrs. Lucile Echoes had a beauty salon in a small building next to her house. Not only were we taught to be creative, but we also saw creativity and entrepreneurship in action from many adults who found a means to survive within a segregated culture.

Children don't always question why things are the way they are. They generally are able to adapt themselves to their circumstances and make the best of it using the imagination that comes from their naiveté. Although our socioeconomic status was not an issue for the children, as an adult I now recognize it had to have been oppressive and demoralizing for our parents and other Black adults.

For sure, despite our poverty, our safety, survival, and education were paramount to our parents. As children, we did not realize the danger we faced daily. Nevertheless, our parents and other community adults knew that many of the things we needed for security and to enhance our chances to succeed in life were not readily available to us. But that did not dampen their drive and determination to gives us opportunities for a better future.

On some occasions, especially on Saturday nights, Ku Klux Klan members donned their trademark hoods and rode through our community flashing their headlights and blowing their car horns. Whenever the word circulated that the KKK was riding, everyone would rush into their homes and close their doors. Sometimes the Klansmen would stop and burn crosses in people's yards. Our parents would not allow us to watch as the Klan members carried out in their wicked rituals. They made sure we were out of sight even as fear gripped our hearts. The next day we would hear about what the Klan had done the previous night. Without question, fear tormented the entire community whenever the KKK took the liberty to terrorize it.

Many of the Black women in the community worked as domestics in the homes of Whites. They cared for their children, cleaned their homes, and cooked their meals, while many of the men did their handiwork, gardening, and repairs.

Restaurants were closed to African Americans, and those businesses that did serve Blacks would cater to them only from a back door or window. African Americans were not permitted to enter through the front door even to purchase take-out meals.

Whenever we happened to travel to Bessemer, we would see water fountains labeled "White" and "Colored." All the salespersons were White, as were all of the bankers, automobile dealers, entrepreneurs and professional people. I recall that some of the elevator operators and custodians were African American, however. We lived in a society where White America did not recognize African Americans as significant contributors to the evolution of the community they lived in, nor did they feel that African Americans should benefit equally from its progress.

Our parents were not high school graduates, but for us, not having an education certainly was not an option. Acquiring knowledge was a priority in our family and in the community. Not only did we have to attend school, we had to perform well and submit to our school's authority. School was the place where we experienced African Americans working in professional capacities.

It was an honor to see Mr. King, the principal, and other male teachers dressed in quality suits and the ladies wearing pretty dresses. They conducted themselves as the professionals they were. It was encouraging to see smart, well-dressed, and well-spoken African Americans in charge of our school's operations and instructions.

At times we would see White men and women talking with the teachers and walking through the buildings and grounds. We knew they were from the Board of Education, but we were not intimidated by their presence. In our home, we received instructions never to fear White people but to respect all people. No one taught us that we were inferior to them, even though we could see the enormous chasm separating the quality of our living conditions. It did not take a genius to see that there was a difference between our standards of living based on skin color.

Although we would pass through White communities and see school playground equipment that we could only dream about and beautiful parks that we could not play in, we didn't feel that it made any of us less of a person. How our teachers taught us this, instilled these principals, and how we maintained them, only God knows.

Thinking about our living conditions and how anyone could draw a direct contrast with that of the majority race, one would wonder why and how we could sustain ourselves under such demoralizing circumstances.

What was it that encouraged our parents and others to maintain their drive to make something better out of nothing?

What moved them to shield us from White adults' negative comments in public places and from their children who clearly had been taught to segregate themselves from us?

What was it that inspired our father to walk miles to a job where he would be humiliated all day long to provide for his family? And how did our parents maintain their self-control with such grace and restraint?

When addressing these questions, we arrive at what one might say is an obvious answer: They knew that things would get better with a deep and abiding faith in God.

What I did not want to do for God is the thesis of this memoir. When I think about the existential condition of African Americans in Dolomite, Alabama, during the 1950s and '60s, they lived under the discriminatory, segregated, and oppressive circumstances of the time. I can only imagine what the people did not want to do. However, they had no choice under the slave police state mentality of White people. I have learned that nobody could have done the things in my life like the Lord, nobody but God! Nobody could have turned the impossible situation of my life around to work for my good, but God.

This book opens with my introduction, focusing on the fact that I never wanted to be a preacher. The biblical character Moses had so many excuses not to do what God was calling him to do. That is how I felt about being called to the ministry. Becoming a pastor was never something that attracted me, and there were so many other things that I thought I wanted to do, and none of them had to do with spiritual or religious participation.

Chapter one details my childhood, growing up in Dolomite, Alabama, and reared by a very compassionate mother and a hard-working, disciplinarian father. The church was automatic in our home, in part because of the times in which we lived.

Church also served as an outlet because African Americans were limited, for many reasons, in the things they could do and the places they could go for fun and entertainment. However, what was more critical to our community was spirituality; the people believed in God.

Chapter two shares some of my experiences after leaving Dolomite and moving out in the world on my own as a young man. Most of the guys in our community left their homes after securing employment in the steel or coal mines industry, or they enlisted in the military. When I moved from

James, Sr. and Mamie King Bryant

Dolomite, I was on my way to college at Tuskegee Institute. Tuskegee was an experience of a lifetime. I received exposure to people and things I never thought possible for African Americans. Experiencing this level of African-American participation in society made me incredibly proud of my people.

This chapter also highlights my employment opportunities after graduating from Tuskegee Institute and looking out into a world that I had never experienced. I have always thought of myself as very versatile, but I had no specific employment plans. I understood from my Dolomite experience that I had to find work to support myself and my family. I never saw myself being above any type of work if it was legal, and I could earn a living wage. I always believed in "ladder climbing," which is starting low and moving upward. So, it did not matter the company if there were opportunities to advance.

Chapter three focuses on my commitment to the church and the extraordinary experience that I believe had the most profound impact on my ministry preparation and God placing me at the Friendship Church. It is a miracle from God that I learned about ITC and gained exposure to Dr. Charles Jackson Sargent. Only God could have created this scenario for me.

Chapter four deals with the vision God gave me that was so authentic that nothing could block my pursuit of its fulfillment. I had never experienced anything so real that had not yet manifested itself in my life. I knew about dreams and visions, but what I experienced was beyond that, and I do not know how to label it. Although I was warned by seasoned ministers not to change anything when initially being called to a church, I was on a mission from God, and my passion was so strong that there was nothing or no one who could take away the vision God gave me. The vision was real!

Chapter five relates my experience with a vicious and ungodly side of the parish ministry—one I had never seen or heard about before. Still, I could see God in all of it to accomplish the mission God called me to do. Through all the ministry trials, I learned that faith in God was all I needed to survive. I never thought that people in the church could do some of the wicked things I saw and experienced. I must admit that it was painful to encounter people who often told me that they loved me, but I could see that they were vigorously seeking to destroy me.

When I questioned why I was going through so many challenges at the church, God assured me that it was Him they were after and not me. I was embarrassed for the church when we found ourselves in courtrooms time after time over ten years, but I could still see God working in my favor. After allowing certain situations to play out, God gave me the signal that it was time to fight back. We indeed fought back, but I got out of the way and let God fight my battles. That was the only way to victory.

Although I became weary of the constant fighting, God encouraged me every step of the way to hang on in there and not grow weary. There were times I felt like Daniel in the lion's den. He was able to sleep among hungry, man-eating lions and was not harmed. Although there were times of weariness, God gave me peace.

Chapter six tells of the vision becoming a reality, and that through it all, God consistently demonstrated we could depend on God. We were

Dr. Donald Bryant with Dr. Gardner C. Taylor

able to build a multi-million-dollar facility debt-free. Although I told the people at the birth of the vision that God's people would finance us, I had no idea how that would happen. But I never doubted God, and God never fails. I share some practical steps in building and becoming debt-free. I never believed that God's Church should be indebted to anyone other than God!

Chapter seven explains the successful transition plan implemented for my successor. I think it is vital that every pastor and leader understands that God uses us only for a season. I have seen too many pastors and leaders hold on to positions and power well beyond their productive years. There are just too many biblical examples. Legacies are made when successors can carry the previous leader's baton. God showed me years ago that I should not hold on to the pastor's position beyond my season. I am thankful to God for me knowing my season. It was my time to leave.

In conclusion, I wrap up my real-life experiences from being born in Dolomite, Alabama, to becoming a successful pastor in a major metropolitan city and leaving a legacy that lifts God through Jesus and Jesus alone.

Donald Earl Bryant
East Point, Georgia

Chapter One
Growing Up in Dolomite, Alabama

Growing up, becoming a preacher was never a profession I aspired to. As I grew into manhood, nothing changed. I was not excited by the possibility when God called me. Preachers were always highly regarded and respected in our community. It was the preacher that everyone looked to for guidance and modeling. In the African-American community in Dolomite, the preacher served as the spokesperson for the community and was on the front line in communicating the empowering and liberating Word of God. The preacher was the center of attention in Dolomite. Every day, people would go to work and take care of their daily chores, but on Sundays, almost 95 percent attended church regularly.

At church, the preacher was on center stage and all eyes were on him. The preacher captured the attention of the people with his compelling presentation and the substance of his message. Amid the difficult life situations in which the people found themselves, they looked forward to hearing from God through the preacher.

I cited those verses from Exodus 4 in the introduction because Moses did not want to take on the assignment to which God was calling him. He said in verse 13 (CSB): "Please, Lord, send someone else."

This is one of many texts where God used people who were not enthusiastic about what God was calling them to do. Moses, being a Hebrew, would

Donald Bryant (middle, front row) with his siblings, father, and aunt

serve as an excellent example to show how God can do extraordinary things through ordinary people, even when they are reluctant participants.

I want to openly share how God used a Dolomite, Alabama man who was not particularly eloquent, diligent, or perfect to draw people from the community. I want to share with you how, amid all my shortcomings and lack of enthusiasm, God used me to lead a church through years of intense conflict, as observed by preachers and church leaders across this country.

I did not want to be a church leader, not to mention being a pastor. It was not something that I wanted to do or ever dreamed of doing. It seemed there was always something else that I would rather have been doing other than being in church. Although I grew up in the church, I never wanted to be a preacher or ever thought I could. Even after I became a minister, I never developed the passion for preaching that other preachers seem to have, even to this day.

When God called Moses from a burning bush, he did not consider himself adequately qualified for the assignment. He suggested that perhaps someone else would be better suited. I, too, felt less than equipped to be a preacher when God called me to ministry.

The first time I had an opportunity to choose whether I was going to church or not, I was eighteen years old and enrolled in college. Growing up in my parents' home, church attendance and participation were requirements. So, when I left home and could make that decision for myself, I chose not to go. I was more impressed by fine clothes, beautiful cars, pretty women, playing football, and going to parties.

Jesus was not my model!

I wanted to be like Ron O'Neal in Super Fly, David Ruffin, Richard Roundtree in Shaft, Smokey Robinson, or some other famous entertainer. As time passed, I found myself farther and farther away from the church.

My life paralleled that of the parable told by Jesus in Luke 15, "The Prodigal Son." I found myself going places and doing things that my family did not model for me at home. I had turned away from seeking the face of God. I was lost!

I had been a wayward son, but I also was very much a reluctant chosen leader. Moses's biblical story leading the Israelites out of captivity in Egypt has always been an exciting story to me. Still, I never thought that my life and ministry would mirror that of Moses. Exodus 4:10–13 captures my call to ministry and the context in which I found myself.

As we have learned, Moses was not born into a royal family, but instead, he was born into slavery, and God positioned him with a royal family to meet divine destiny. Moses, reared in an Egyptian home by the Pharaoh's daughter, had all the perks of a privileged child. Pharaoh's daughter took him in and loved and nurtured him. It took some time for God to manifest in Moses' life. He was 80 years old before the call of God from a burning bush became a reality in his life, and he embraced his identity as a Hebrew and rejected the opportunity to be privileged while his people were suffering at the hand of the Egyptian government.

In this chapter of Exodus, God spoke to Moses through a burning bush that was not consumed by the fire, and that was a supernatural experience for Moses to see. As God spoke and challenged Moses to lead, Moses found every excuse not to accept the call of God. Moses felt that he should not be the one to perform the task that God was assigning him. Or maybe other commitments in his personal life were more important. He did not have any history that suggests that he could confront the Pharaoh of Egypt on behalf of God, who was calling for the release of the Hebrew slaves.

Moses used another excuse that he was not eloquent in speaking, as if God was not aware of his gifts. What I have learned about Moses and myself is that all we can bring to the ministry table is ultimately a willing spirit to trust God. What we now know is that Moses was remarkably successful at what God was calling him to do.

At the time, success was not a word that Moses would have embraced, nor would I have adopted that word in my formative years and indeed not early in my ministry as a pastor. But now, as I reflect on the church work God gave me, I must say as humbly as I know how, through it all, God blessed me with a very successful ministry.

Although the preacher was highly regarded in our community, becoming a preacher was never what I wanted to pursue as a career goal. The preacher had the ear of all the people, and he was considered the most influential person in the community. The preacher was always well dressed, well-spoken, and often drove a nice car. My family's history is void of preachers in our lineage, which would suggest that preachers were not likely in future generations. The closest models for my life were my father and my brother, and neither were preachers.

My father was a stable and respected ironworker in the community known by many as "Tit and Dolomite" and he served as assistant superintendent of Sunday School. My brother, "Bug," was the firstborn and very popular in the community and at school.

He played tenor saxophone in the high school band and quarterback on the football team, and I wanted to be just like him. These two figures were most influential in my childhood and adolescent years. Becoming a preacher was the furthest thing from my mind.

My mother's father, Robert King, Sr., was a deacon in the church, while at the same time, he owned a little community store next to his home with a barbershop and sold moonshine. Allegedly in 1929, he had slot machines in Dolomite; he was indeed a hustler who cared for his family, the community, and the church. Years ago, I learned from one of my grandfather's contemporaries that his entrepreneurial activities caused the deacons to have a called meeting about his ethical behavior, then tabled it. He died in 1955, with the discussion still on the table.

My mother's brother William (Uncle "Po Bill") King was a pure joker. He once said, "When I was promoted to the second grade, I was too nervous to shave."

One Saturday night while drinking moonshine, my grandfather's son, James ("Jim Wolf") took the family dog out to the church and baptized it in the church's outdoor baptismal pool. But that did not stop the baptism service the next day because it took days to fill the baptismal pool.

My father's brother Charlie ("Charlie D") worked in the coal mine, and every day he would faithfully go to work. He was our favorite uncle because he always gave us money, but on weekends he would get sloppy drunk—I mean sloppy drunk—you could see him on the side of the road, lying in a pathway or lying in someone's yard. But when Monday came, he was ready for work, and not until Friday would he have another drink and start his weekend drinking spree.

One Sunday morning, Uncle Charlie D joined Saint John Baptist Church; he was drunk when he walked down the church aisle to accept Christ. Ever since that day, he never took another drink, and he became such a trusted member of the church. They voted him to become the church treasurer. He was good with numbers because he also prepared taxes for a few people. Uncle Charlie D held the position of church treasurer faithfully until his health began to fail. I saw firsthand what believing in God could do, but it did not influence me to seek God at the time; indeed, it didn't. Uncle Charlie D died a short time later from lung cancer while living at Momma Rosa's house—his mother, and our grandmother.

During that time, Dolomite was like all the African-American communities in the area. Travel was limited and restricted and many of the white neighborhoods were off-limits. Parks, swimming pools, and other recreational activities were not available to us even though most men worked and paid taxes for those facilities but were not permitted to use them.

During my teenage years, the older guys worked and were able to buy cars and homes. It was the accumulation of things that made one feel as if he or she was progressing. Our success was made evident by our educational achievements, work statuses, and material possessions.

Johnny Scott went on to become a medical doctor. U.W. Clemons became a lawyer, and then he became a Justice on Alabama's Supreme Court. Kenneth Epps became a Lt. Colonel in the US Navy. There were also several males and female teachers from Dolomite. My brother James, Jr. became a supervisor for US Steel and later started his own construction company. It is easy to see that serving the Lord in Dolomite, Alabama was not in vain.

Night clubs were trendy and familiar places. The clubs were either in a room in a residential home or a standalone building. All the club owners appeared to be very wealthy because they lived in beautiful homes and drove expensive cars. For the most part, people got along very well in Dolomite. However, almost every weekend, we would hear about fights at clubs. There was always a fight somewhere, either in Dolomite or adjoining little towns. For the most part, the violence happened at clubs and other places called "shot houses." These were where illegal alcohol was sold and consumed.

Domestic abuse happened but was not commonplace. While I'm sure our parents didn't tell us children everything that happened in the community, from my perspective, the people of Dolomite got along very well. Neighbors were neighbors and they were there for each other's needs if they were able to accommodate them.

Mrs. Penny and Mr. H. built a block building, which to us, was like a grocery store.

Mrs. Sue had a big store that looked like today's 7-ELEVEN®, and these stores seemed to be perfectly placed around in the community.

Miss Dora had a room in her house stacked with can goods, tobacco products, and candy. The people of Dolomite did what they could do to live and move their families forward.

These were everyday people doing there best to provide for their families and contribute positively to their communities. It is this small, nurturing community that gave me a foundation to venture into the world.

Early Church Life

In our community, there were approximately eight churches, including Baptist, Pentecostal, Methodists, and Church of God. Our family was members of the Saint John Baptist Church in Happy Hollow, another area in the community, about one mile north of our home.

The pastor was L. N. Clark. He lived in Tuscaloosa, Alabama, and commuted to Dolomite twice a month. Pastor Clark was a very handsome and well-groomed man who had a smooth delivery with a very distinctive "hoop." The people loved him. I enjoyed seeing him and listening to him, and there were times when he would bring a young boy about my age (Freddie) with him, and we became friends. I looked forward to seeing Freddie, and we would sit together during church services. When our family served dinner for the preacher, Freddie and I would eat together and spend a little time playing outside after dinner.

The church is where we learned about God and Jesus, where people held on to hope and faith that racist and discriminatory behavior could not take away. It was in Dolomite's churches where the adults could be who God intended them to be, not what an oppressive, racist society wanted them to be.

The church is where the same African-American man who was called the n-word all week by Whites, was addressed on Sunday as Mr. Chairman. Rather than being called "Girl" or "Gal," and "Boy," the people were called Mrs., Miss, Mother, Sister, and Brother in the church and community.

In the church, women were not disrespected but instead respected as great women of God. The church nurtured men and women to become leaders in the community. They were examples for the younger people to follow. Deacons Henry Dean, George Taylor, Louis Lucas (Boy Scout leader), "Big Will" Harris (Farmer), George Forrest (Social Action), "Little Dad" Johnson (Athletics), Joe Debose, Candy Green, John Hudson and

J. W. Hudson (community organizers) and others played essential roles in the life and development of the Dolomite community.

Some men gave of themselves to help the entire community though they had families themselves. Mrs. Belle Debose, Nellie Layfield, Hanna McBride, Jessie Mealing (teacher), Ruby Lee Sanders (teacher), and other women provided public support in cooperation with the men.

Finally, the church brought the meager resources of a deprived community together to accomplish great things. Together faith, hope, and love became a reality in the community shunned by the political and social powers in control.

The children were introduced to the church by family members and friends. The church provided an opportunity to get to know God personally and a chance to learn and practice survival skills. Critical to the children's survival was discipline. The adults expected children to put on their best behavior at church. There was no running around out of control at the church. There were structured activities for boys, girls, and families.

Children could learn to recite speeches and improve their reading, speaking, and writing skills. The church meant even more for our parents. For our parents and other adults, the church was a refuge. It was the place where they could "lay their burdens down" and hear the preacher tell them a fiery message about a God who can change their condition. They were encouraged and taught about a God who loves them and loves them no less than anyone else.

In many African-American homes, there was a picture of a White Jesus kneeling and praying. Very few people thought that image was Jesus because the photograph did not look like them but somewhat resembled the persons who abused and oppressed them daily. It was in the church where the reality of good and evil revealed itself.

The preaching of the Gospel inspired people to believe that God would change things if they trusted God and did their part. The elders in the community understood what the Germans called *Sitz im Leben*, or the sociological context of their situation in life, even though the children were oblivious to it.

Our parents knew that someone could get killed when the Ku Klux Klan drove through the community, and nothing would ever happen to the KKK. African Americans knew that educational, social, and economic opportunities were in their midst but denied.

Through the church, groups organized to enhance the community in which they lived. Men and women were able to network and share whatever ideas and resources they had. The community understood that involvement in the church would increase their chances of getting jobs and finding favor with all humanity.

As children, we would hear from our elders how the preacher really preached and how well the choir sang during services. People were proud of the things they did at church and held each other in high esteem.

Although there were several churches and denominations in the community, at some point during the month, almost everyone had the opportunity to worship with other churches. Chicken dinners and fish sandwiches were sold on occasion to raise money to support a cause or ministry aspect. Those events also presented opportunities for interdenominational fellowship within the community.

I was able to see and experience so many people in the community with the churches. We were in church every Sunday, not because that is where I wanted to be, but because our parents demanded our participation.

I remember one Sunday I was not feeling well. When I told my father I was ill, he said that I did not have to go to church that day. When the family left for church, I started to feel better. By the time my family returned from church services, I was not feeling sick at all.

My friends Mack, FD, Bobby, and other guys were playing football on the back street, and I asked my father if I could go out back and play with them. He said to me, "Oh, no! Donald, you are sick!" I was not permitted to leave the house at all that day.

Our household fully participated in the church. My parents were not fanatics but were dedicated and consistent. My brother and sisters were extremely disciplined, and our parents always welcomed church leaders asking us to participate in different programs. They would ask us because they knew we would say yes, and we were rather good at what we did.

If there were plays, presentations, or speeches, we had to participate. Often, the adults would boast to my parents about how well I did something at the church. I remember one lady saying to me, "God is going to make a preacher out of you." Those words went right over my head, and I never gave it a second thought.

At the time I entered high school, my brother "Bug" had a part-time job cleaning the office of Dr. John W. Nixon, a dentist and president of the NAACP branch in Ensley, Alabama. I inherited that cleaning job when I was in the tenth grade and worked there two evenings a week throughout high school.

My father would always drive me to work, and I remember the day that Dr. Nixon came rushing out of his office with a terrifying voice, saying, "They have killed Dr. King!" That is where I was on April 4, 1968, cleaning the dentist's office after school. That was a tragic day I will never forget.

In high school, I continued to do well in my studies, church, and community. I also played quarterback for the Westfield High School Wildcats football team, as had my brother, during my junior and senior years. Mack Walker, a particularly good friend, taught me how to throw a football with power and accuracy.

James, Sr. and Mamie Bryant and Family
(Donald is pictured far right, back row)

Mack was a couple of years older, and I would ride with him and his girlfriend, Mary Faye, and visit funeral homes to look at the dead. Mack also taught me how to dance with girls.

By my senior year in high school, I was the starting quarterback for our football team. I don't want to brag, but I was good, and our team was incredible.

My father came home from work one Friday, and I had not completed the work he'd told me to finish that day. When he saw that I had not finished, he told me that I couldn't play in the game our team had scheduled that night. I couldn't believe it! I was the starting quarterback and this was an important game. We had to win this game to receive an invitation to play in the Turkey Bowl Classic, the biggest sporting event for African Americans in the Birmingham area. More than fifteen thousand people would attend that game on Thanksgiving Day.

When my father gave me work to do, he expected me to get it done, and done right. He would tell us often, "If you do a job right the first time, you will not have to do it again." I did not complete the assignment he gave me, so that meant I did not do it right. The word got out that my father would not let me play that evening (I think my mother told someone). Coach Robert Dickerson came to our house, and he and my father talked in the yard for a long time. After they finished, my father told me that would be allowed to play in the game that evening, but he reminded me of the work I still needed to finish.

What I learned from my father is a work ethic that proved to be invaluable. This life lesson has been a tremendous asset in every area of my life. Later, I would find just how vital that ethic would prove to be in building a significant ministry.

Chapter Two
Growing into Manhood

A fter my senior year football season, I received several college football scholarships, and I decided to attend Tuskegee Institute (now Tuskegee University). I believe my parents, especially my mother, wanted me to enroll in Tuskegee because Tee Tee's daughter, Betty, lived in the city of Tuskegee with her husband, Jay Gould Williams.

On August 18, 1968, I enrolled in Tuskegee Institute. It marked the first time I had stayed away from my hometown of Dolomite. I had never left Alabama's boundaries, neither had I ridden on a bus or flown on an airplane.

My freshman year in college opened opportunities for me to ride a bus, fly on an airplane, and travel outside of Alabama. But more than that, when I moved to Tuskegee, it was the first time I saw African Americans in positions of authority. I saw an African-American mayor, a university president, a county sheriff and sheriff's deputies, bankers, grocery store owners, an automobile dealer, and service station owners.

For the first eighteen years of my life, I had not experienced this level of African-American involvement and empowerment in a community. Arriving at Tuskegee was indeed a culture shock for an 18-year-old teenager from Dolomite. I fell in love with Tuskegee because I saw in real-time what my father had told me most of my life, "You can be whatever you want to be."

As a freshman at Tuskegee, I was able to choose whether I wanted to attend church or not. My older cousins, Jay and Betty Williams, were nurses at the VA hospital. Both attended Saint Paul Methodist Church, and I attended church services with them a couple of times. But after that, I decided to hang out with the fellows on campus and party every chance I got. During this time, I drifted far away from the church. Football occupied most of my time; the rest of my time was for me. I met some guys from the Bessemer and Birmingham area and became good friends with them. Orlando, Belser, Bruce, Clinton, Zeke, Leslie ("Super Chicken"), and I were incredibly close because we lived in the same dormitory and were from the same area.

Jerome Hadden and I were football teammates at Westfield. He also earned a football scholarship. Jerome was the best tailback I had seen in person. He reminded me of the excellent NFL star Gale Sayers. Jerome and I were roommates, and all of us guys were very close.

Bruce, Belser, and Orlando were active members of the Catholic Church, but I never recall them going to mass in Tuskegee. Leslie married a preacher's daughter our junior year; however, we never attended church with them.

These guys helped me adjust to the away-from-home experience. Belser and Orlando were brothers whose parents had bought them a new car, as had Bruce's parents. There were enough students with automobiles that I could hitchhike around Tuskegee with ease. I never had to worry about transportation.

Beginning freshman classes was a new and exciting phase of my life experience. I was fortunate to have participated in the Freshman Experimental Program (FEP). The FEP gave me the grace I needed not to flunk out of school. It was a unique program designed to assist freshmen in the transition from high school to college. I didn't know how to "do" college, and that first year was so important for me to get a real understanding of what college was all about. I was so uninformed that I did not know what "major" meant. I heard some of the fellows say something about political science, so I placed political science on my registration form, having no idea what was involved in that field of study.

My first indication that God might be doing something outstanding in my life regarding the church happened on the steps of my dormitory, Emory IV. I stood on the steps and began to mimic a preacher in a worship service with about ten guys standing around. With the Bible in my hand, I spoke from God's Word. I cannot remember what I said, but the act itself now rings with significance in my memory. After that experience, however, I continued in my wayward lifestyle and my newfound habits. No more church; life was just fun, fun, fun!

After making it through my freshman year and learning more about the college experience, I became more intentional as a college student. I met Mr. Harvey Mirsky, a graduate of the University of Chicago who taught marketing. He impressed me in his class, and he encouraged me to consider a career in marketing after I graduated.

At the beginning of my second year, I declared a new major, business management, with an emphasis on marketing. Although I still didn't know what I wanted to do after college, I concluded that a business background would help, regardless of my career objectives.

I have always been a worker, and although I was enrolled in college, I was no different there. I did not have a lot of time to work, however, considering playing football and schoolwork. Nevertheless, I was able to secure a part-time job thanks to my cousins Jay and Betty. They were friends with Bill Childs, who owned a Chevron Service Station on Highway 80, just down the street. Bill hired me to work ten hours a week.

Bill was the brother of Jean Childs, the first wife of Andrew Young, former UN ambassador and mayor of Atlanta. My work ethic kicked in during my employment with Bill. He was pleased with my performance while I was amazed at working for an African American who owned a service station.

During my sophomore year, I got kicked off the football team when I bumped into the head football coach, Leroy Smith, in the business office with a cigarette in my mouth. This incident ended my scholarship. I was third on the depth chart at the time, so I was not disappointed.

I applied for a student loan and was approved to pay for tuition and fees. My schoolwork did not suffer, and I did not miss a beat. I just was not playing football. And yes, I paid off my student loan. Although I worked part-time, my school life took a more deliberate direction during my junior and senior years. I began to make the dean's list, and I frequented the library and the classroom. I was still young, so my social life did not take a total hit. At the time, the Commodores were a hot music group on campus, and there were other entertainers and sporting events—football, basketball, baseball, and tennis matches—that took place on campus.

On weekends, my friends and I would go to the Black Forest Club where the Commodores with Lionel Richie and the DuPonts with Tom Joyner performed. They were all students at Tuskegee. There were times when my friends and I had opportunities to get on stage with them. Entertainers such as the Bar-Kays, Delphonics, Funkadelics, and others came to Tuskegee to perform in Logan Hall. Tuskegee was the place to be socially, and although I enjoyed it, I did not drift from my studies. Oddly, Tuskegee did not have a reputation for its social life. The world knew Tuskegee for its engineering, nursing, business, agriculture, and veterinary medicine schools.

Before I graduated, my girlfriend Diane and I had a son who was born September 3, 1971, in Montgomery. I was not prepared for fatherhood. I had no idea what it meant to be a father and, for sure, not a responsible father. I had no clue! I could not afford to buy a diaper or a pair of boxer shorts. How could I support a family?

Although I had experienced my father's role in the family, I never picked up on the details of how he did it. I learned how to work from my father, but I did not know how to care for a family as he had done.

Upon graduating from Tuskegee in May 1972, I returned to Dolomite and got married to my son's mother—without my parents' knowledge. I'm certain they were dismayed that I didn't inform them of my intentions to marry Diane, but they never expressed their disappointment.

I guess they were wise enough to know that there was nothing they could do at that point except support my decision. My parents were genuine people; they met Diane's family and were very amicable toward them. Our parents visited with one another, and both families did what they could to support our little family. Donald II was their grandson, and they embraced and loved him.

Pursuing a Career

About a month after I graduated from Tuskegee in 1972, I got a job with the Jefferson County Committee for Equal Opportunity (JCCEO) as a summer camp supervisor. I worked on that job in Birmingham over the summer, and when that program ended, I searched for other opportunities.

That September, I moved to Jamaica, New York, with my cousin Joseph Smith, a detective with the New York Police Department. My wife and our young son stayed with her parents. Joseph's brothers, Benjamin and Robert, also lived in Jamaica, and worked for Eastern Airlines. It was my hope when leaving Dolomite that I could secure employment with Eastern.

After several months working at a department store in Manhattan, Benjamin scheduled a meeting for me with Eastern Airlines human resources. I secured employment on December 4, 1972, as a ramp serviceman. I worked at John F. Kennedy International Airport and I still remember Gate 17 because one day it was so cold that I cried. The severe weather hurt! I did not like living in New York, not so much due to the cold, but because people did not seem friendly. Building relationships was hard. The only people I knew who were my age worked for Eastern.

I was not homesick, but the people's attitudes in New York and Alabama were so vastly different. My mother's younger brother, Samuel King, also lived in Brooklyn, and we would see each other and socialize on occasions. My father's brother, Lee Bryant, lived in Manhattan, but I only saw him once. None of my New York family were devout churchgoers, so attending worship was not a part of my New York experience.

About six months after I was hired at Eastern, the opportunity came for me to transfer with Eastern to Atlanta. In June 1973, I relocated to Atlanta, and that move was like heaven to me. Nine months in the "Big Apple" was more than enough.

I was ecstatic to leave New York for several reasons. First, I did not click with New Yorkers. I had a difficult time adjusting to the New York lifestyle. Second, I truly wanted to return to the South and a warmer climate. Third, the people in Atlanta were much more approachable and extremely friendly. Compared to New York, Atlanta was like heaven to me. Also, my marriage had been annulled, so there was no reason for me to return to Dolomite.

During my employment with Eastern Airlines, as a single man, my involvement with women and social indiscretions were what consumed my days. My life model was not Jesus, but rather playboys and movie stars.

The early 1970s was a turbulent time for boomers and hippies. Many temptations promised a panacea for my life. I purchased a new silver Datsun 240Z, and when I got settled in Atlanta, I soon realized that experimenting with all the things that were supposed to bring joy and happiness brought nothing of the sort. At best, the pleasure was short-lived. During this period, I remained separate from God; however, I attended church services on occasion, but not for worship.

Being a well-dressed young man with a fancy new sports car, living in a penthouse, and carrying a few dollars in my pockets, I was still very immature and had no real time for God or anything else that was good for my life. I lived like I did not have a care in the world and no responsibility outside of myself.

My mother often would remind me that I had a son and needed to spend time with him. I did bring Donald II over to Atlanta a couple of times. We even flew to Orlando to visit Disney World, but the trip was not as exciting as I thought it would have been.

Our father-son relationship was lukewarm even though he was a small child. I am convinced that we had a dysfunctional relationship because of my inability to function as a father. I am indeed grateful to his mother and grandparents, uncles, and aunts for their involvement in his growth and development.

As I continued my young adult journey, God showed up and revealed something to me at Eastern Airlines that took me back to church. I noticed that even in Atlanta, with all the great African-American colleges and universities, and educated Black residents, Eastern Airlines had very few African Americans in managerial positions.

Furthermore, the employees' racial makeup was so out of balance that it moved me to action. Eastern was a good company with fair wages, health benefits, flying privileges, and other perks. White men without high school diplomas came to Atlanta from the country after working on their farms and worked at the airport. They would unload and load an airplane or two, and then returned to their farms—their time and pay reflected a full eight hours, and sometimes overtime.

But opportunities in every area of the company were lacking for African Americans. At Eastern, I did not meet one African-American employee who did not have at least a high school diploma, and most were college graduates. I first went to my immediate supervisor to express my concerns, and he directed me to human resources to communicate what I thought were inequities in hiring and promotion practices.

Later, I wrote a letter to the department head in Atlanta and copied the CEO, Colonel Frank Borman, the former astronaut, based in Miami. I continued to raise awareness about inequities wherever I could, among co-workers, flight attendants, mechanics, aircraft cleaners, and others.

The word got back to management, and I received a notice to meet with the director of human resources in Atlanta. In that second meeting, I shared my observations and expressed concerns. Believe it or not, I received an offer for a management position. But I wasn't falling for that. I explained that I was not interested in a management position to satisfy myself. I wanted to see African Americans move into areas of employment that were equal to their White counterparts.

A few weeks later, Colonel Borman came to Atlanta and wanted to meet with me. In that meeting, I explained the conditions on the ground related to Atlanta's hiring and promotion practices. He promised me that some future action would correct the problem. The next day I met with the human resources director, and he asked what I thought the company should do.

I told him that I was willing to go into the African-American community and seek qualified people to work for Eastern. The old narrative said that "qualified" African-American candidates were hard to find. He then gave me a stack of employment applications, and I was to report back to him within two weeks. I decided to share that information with the community. I started with the Jackson Memorial Baptist Church on Fairburn Road in Atlanta.

I met with Pastor Gregory Sutton, who allowed me to announce during worship services regarding openings at Eastern Airlines. The people received this information gladly. I continued to spread the word with Pastor Jasper Williams and with community centers that Eastern was looking for qualified African Americans to fill several positions.

I used my apartment at Cedar Woods to pick up applications and re-turn them as soon as possible. I did not expect quick results. Within one month, I submitted more than twenty applications.

Eight people were hired from the applications I submitted—flight attendants, ramp agents, and cleaners. Although I did not think that this effort produced the desired outcome, they hired people, and the spotlight shined on Eastern's promotion and hiring practices. I was out front and leading an effort that would not benefit me, but I was interested and concerned for others' benefit and welfare. Although I did not realize it at the time, God was preparing me to serve others. My mother was a very caring person, and perhaps I had picked up some of her supportive and merciful traits. Indeed, not applied in every area, but as the saying goes, "God was not yet finished with me."

A couple of years later, a desire to go into business arrested my attention. I had moved back to Dolomite in 1980, and my brother-in-law, Clarence Jones, was an entertainment manager who lived in Huntsville. He promoted several well-known groups, including Frankie Beverly and Maze, the Commodores, the Gap Band, Confunkshun, Sherell, and Montenegro.

The idea of a limousine service had become of interest after I met a Huntsville man named Mr. Battle. At the time, I was working with Alfonzo Dawson Funeral Home in Atlanta. Since my days as a teenager, funeral homes were interesting to me, and I wanted to learn more about the practical aspects of the business.

Mr. Dawson had a fleet of beautiful two-toned burgundy and beige limousines, and he and I got along exceptionally well. I talked with Clarence and let him know that I had access to some sharp limousines, and maybe he could allow me to start a service with him.

Clarence was booking Ashford and Simpson and Stephanie Mills for the Atlanta Civic Center, and he allowed me to service them. I got two other guys to work with me—one of them had limousine experience, and the other guy was there to help with VIP service. We were dressed in tuxedos and offered an excellent service to our clients. Clarence was incredibly pleased. I was excited about a hot start, and it resulted in a remarkably successful limousine business. This service also attracted a crowd that did not help me move closer to God. If anything, the industry moved me even further away, or so I thought.

One Saturday night I was in a Birmingham nightclub. There was a young group performing, and they were excellent. After they finished, I talked with them as the club was closing. During the conversation, I dropped Clarence, Quinton, and WG's names for obvious reasons. Everyone in the industry knew them. So, the group invited me to one of their band rehearsals held at one of their parent's homes.

Shortly after that night, I became the group's manager. After a few engagements and heightened trust among us, I wanted to change the group's name. I always wanted a Mercedes Benz car, so I influenced them to change their name to Benz. The name helped enhance their visibility, and I was able to get them on stage as an opening act for Confunkshun, Gap Band, and many engagements in clubs.

Bob Dickerson arranged to highlight the name Benz on the Birmingham Civic Center marquee for a couple of weeks. They got so good they thought they no longer needed me as a manager. They were persuaded to sign with another manager and went to New York to record a song. The music scene never heard from this band again. Meanwhile, I continued to oblige other entertainers with the limousine service.

After some time traveling through the states and mixing and mingling with top entertainers, one would have thought that a young man would be satisfied. Yet I had an unfulfilled void, an itch yet unscratched. My lifestyle afforded me a degree of notoriety, money, and beautiful women, but loneliness and a feeling of emptiness overshadowed it all.

One weekend in November 1983, we had a break from touring with groups. I returned to Dolomite, and there I was, home alone. God came to me in my hour of loneliness and emptiness. With tears in my eyes, what I had been taught from my childhood became real. I needed God in my life; God was my only hope. Nothing else had been able to fill the void in the lifestyle that I had engaged in for years.

Had it not been for my upbringing in the church, that night could have been a tragedy. If I had not called on the God of my parents and community, my life might have ended that night. God, thank You. The Lord had been with me for those years at home with my parents and remains with me until this present day. As a boy "forced" to attend church, and running from God as a young man, this same man was now earnestly seeking the face of God. It was that night when things changed in my life. After engaging in a wayward lifestyle for almost fifteen years, the end of that road was nearing.

On that night in Dolomite, I made a confession and a commitment to God. Now, it was time to get to know God—the same God who had been talked about all my life and who unknowingly had been with me all my days. I told God that night, "If I live one more day or one more week, month, or year… whatever time I have left on this earth, Lord, I will live for you!"

Another significant event took place in my life that was a critical step to making my way back to God. I started working with a one-person contractor, Hinton "Buddy" Johnson, one of my brother's friends. We were doing small jobs like remodeling homes, drywall installations, and room additions. I had done similar work with my brother Bug, and my father always had me doing projects around the house.

Hinton was an active member of Saint John Baptist Church in Happy Hallow, where his younger brother Carl had become pastor. Saint John is where I remember my family first being members.

Hinton was the church's musician; more importantly, he was a tremendous witness to me. Every day as we worked together, he would sing church songs and talk about the goodness of the Lord. I was a good worker with him and took advantage of every opportunity to help him complete his contracted work. He spoke about the church all the time. I believe that God used him to keep the church on my mind as I learned more about construction along the way.

One day my father saw me riding on the back of Buddy's pickup truck with a load of trash. We were taking it to the dump. When I saw my father the next day, he said that I looked "bad" riding on the back of that truck with a college degree. He was disappointed. But I did not see, nor did my father understand, that God was using that experience to grow me. Hinton played a significant role in my developing a positive perception of the church. He did not have to impress me, and there was no need to put on a front. His witness was genuine. He was real.

God became real in my life. At age thirty-three, God stepped into my life and made me a new creation. I left the limousine business and other ungodly engagements in my past. My family had moved their membership years before to New Bethlehem Baptist Church, located about three-quarters of a mile from our home. I was at the Sunday worship service because of the change in my life. When the pastor extended the invitation to unite with the church, I accepted. That was December 25, 1983, and Pastor Daniel Dixon said to me publicly, "Not only do we celebrate Christ's birth today, but we also celebrate your new birth."

That evening my father said to me, "Donald, you have done the right thing. You don't have to worry about anything now."

After uniting with New Bethlehem Baptist Church, we scheduled a baptism date. I had been baptized at age eleven, but I thought it was important that I be re-baptized and invite everyone to my baptism. I thought this was a good thing to do because I had accepted Christ, and by telling everyone, it pushed me to be truthful to my commitment. I now had "skin in the game" and could not turn back. Because of my commitment to the Lord, Bible study, Sunday school, and worship services became a part of my new life. To embrace my new life, God instructed me to move away from the people I had been hanging around. I started associating with others who knew God. Many of my new friends from the community were older people in their fifties, sixties, and even seventies.

After a short period of continually talking with the Lord, I believed without a doubt that God was calling me to be a preacher. There were several elderly ministers in the community, and we often talked about the mysteries of God. On one occasion, when the Bible became confusing for me, I walked to Pastor Spencer Taylor's home and shared my concerns with him. He sat down with his Bible turned to Acts 8:26–40, which emphasizes the need to be taught.

One evening I was visiting my cousin Michael on his farm located south of Birmingham. As we talked and enjoyed each other's company, I noticed one of his neighbors in the distance. The 87-year-old lady was sitting near her well. Having been inspired to go down and speak with her, she shared with me some important things related to God and God's relationship with people. Near the end of our conversation, she said, "I believe that you are a prophet." I considered her words to be confirmation of my call. In my spiritual walk, I have learned that God speaks not only through the Word and nature but also everyday people. As I returned to my cousin's house, the old lady's words encouraged me and stayed with me.

Convinced beyond a doubt that God was calling me to preach, I told my father and he approved. He informed me that he believed God had been calling me for a while. My mother, on the other hand, said, "Donald Earl, I want you to be a good Christian, but I don't want you to be a preacher."

My mother had seen the poor treatment of many preachers. She saw how they were talked about in the community and she did not want to see her son go through that experience. I told her, "Momma, I have to do what God is calling me to do."

Some weeks later, after speaking with Pastor Dixon, he announced to the church that the Lord had called me to preach the Gospel. When the church received the notification, the people responded with a sound of approval and joy.

They made me feel like I was not only accepted as one of God's preachers, but I honestly felt that they welcomed me back home. I made the decision, and now there was no turning back.

The pastor scheduled my initial sermon for April 1, 1984, at 3:00 p.m. It was a joy to tell all the people I knew that the Lord had called me to preach. I told everyone! Every person I knew learned what the Lord was doing in me. I was so excited—it was a great day by all accounts. The church was filled, and people from all around were there. A good friend and contemporary of my father, Deacon Benjamin Hudson, also was preaching his initial sermon that day. After I delivered my sermon at 3:00 p.m., Deacon Hudson preached his sermon at 4:00 p.m.

My sermon text came from 2 Corinthians 5:17 (RSV): *"Therefore, if anyone is in Christ, he is a new creation; the old has passed away, behold, the new has come."* My sermon title was "A New Creature." In that sermon, I talked about how God had changed my life and made me a new creature! Most people in attendance knew that the Lord had brought me out of a world of sin. Although my parents had a good reputation in Dolomite, their baby boy had strayed.

But God!

That evening Brother Hudson and I each received our license to preach the Gospel of Jesus Christ! He and I became even closer as friends and would study together and talk about the power of God. We often met at Hardee's for coffee and biscuits. Sometimes we sat on his porch, sharing our excitement about what God was doing. Minister Hudson's children were my age, and a couple of them were younger, but I was closer to him than I was to his children.

After thirty-three years of human experiences, I was licensed to preach the Gospel of Jesus Christ!

Chapter Three
A Death, a Birth, and a New Life

In June 1984, Mrs. Ruby Epps, a neighbor and dear friend of the family, passed away. Mrs. Epps had played an incredibly important role in my personal development. She lived on the street behind my parents, and when I was a teenager, she often hired me for small jobs, thus allowing me to use my gifts and understand the responsibility involved in working on a home.

Mrs. Ruby and her husband, Mr. Willie, had seven children. All of them were older than me except their son Bruce. Mrs. Epps would pay me to do odd jobs at their home. She trusted me as a teenager to do the work that most young people my age could not do or were not interested in doing (e.g., painting, hanging wallpaper, building a doghouse and similar projects).

It is incredible to look back and see how God used her death to shape my ministerial destiny. I took special note of the fact that my brother and other boys in the community worked for White people—cutting their grass and doing other chores around their houses. My father would never allow me to work for them. If I ever asked him why I could not work at White folks' homes, I don't remember his response. I must also note it was not commonplace at the time for children to question adults, and definitely not my father. Still, I never understood why he would allow Bug to work for them and not me.

Mr. and Mrs. Epps' son, Joe Louis, attended Morehouse School of Religion at the Interdenominational Theological Center (ITC) in Atlanta. He was a friend to Dr. G. Murray Branch, an Old Testament professor at ITC and pastor of the historic Dexter Avenue King Memorial Baptist Church in Montgomery, Alabama.

Dr. Branch came to Dolomite from Montgomery to attend Mrs. Epps' funeral service. Joe Louis introduced me to Dr. Branch as a family friend who recently had received his license to preach. During our conversation, Dr. Branch told me about ITC and the Morehouse School of Religion (MSR) and he suggested that I investigate enrolling.

That same day, he invited me to preach at Dexter Avenue King Memorial Baptist Church in July. What an impressive move of God! Two months after preaching my initial sermon, I had received an invitation to preach at the church where Dr. Martin Luther King, Jr. served as pastor and orchestrated the world-famous Montgomery Bus Boycott.

When New Bethlehem Baptist Church learned that I had received an invitation to Dexter Avenue, they were excited for me. On the Sunday I was to preach, several New Bethlehem members wanted to offer support and be a part of that experience. Some even made the one hundred-mile drive to Montgomery to be with me. It was indeed a wonderful experience!

A month later, August 1984, I enrolled at ITC to pursue a Master of Divinity degree. While a student there, I served as president of the Baptist Student Fellowship, student representative of admissions, and preached at the Morehouse School of Religion's Founders' Day at the ITC chapel.

Another incredibly significant event took place shortly after enrolling at the ITC. One fortuitous day, I was reacquainted with Brenda Williams, a young lady I'd met in 1972 at a McDonald's restaurant on Main Street in East Point, Georgia. She and some co-workers had walked down to the restaurant to have lunch. I just happened to be there that day and we met. We began dating thereafter. She was a telephone operator for Southern Bell, and I was working for Eastern Airlines. For whatever reason, we didn't stay together when we were younger, but after I returned to Atlanta, we started dating again, and the relationship soon moved to commitment. We decided to get married on her birthday, August 29, 1984.

We got married at the beginning of my first semester at the Morehouse School of Religion. I asked the dean, Dr. Edward Wheeler, to marry us in his office. When we got to his office around 10:00 a.m., he asked if I had a suit and if Brenda had a Sunday dress. We told him yes; he then asked us to come back at 2:00 p.m.

Dr. Edward L. Wheeler officiated the wedding of Brenda Lee Williams and Donald Earl Bryant, August 29, 1984

When we came back at 2:00 p.m., Dr. Wheeler had arranged a wedding celebration for us in Bennett Hall. My best man was Brother Allen R. Horton. Brenda's bridesmaid was Mrs. Thelma Johnson. Everett Newton sang, Charles Lewter played the piano, and Thurman Thomas took photographs.

The office staff, along with other students, were present for the occasion and the reception that followed. It was an awe-inspiring experience and something we'd never expected. It seemed as if Dr. Wheeler did not leave out a thing. They had even decorated with flowers. It was just an incredibly special day for us, and one that we will never forget.

I wanted to give Dr. Wheeler twenty-five dollars as a token, but he would not accept a dime. He congratulated us and wished us well. We will forever be grateful to Dr. Wheeler for making that day so special for us.

The Door to Friendship Opens

After the wedding, I settled into marriage, ministry, and matriculation at ITC. One of my professors was Dr. Charles Jackson Sargent, who taught sermon preparation and Baptist Polity at ITC. He also was pastor of the Friendship Baptist Church of College Park.

College Park is two miles west of the Hartsfield-Jackson International airport, known to be the busiest airport in world. This suburban city is just seven miles south of downtown Atlanta, where Booker T. Washington made his historic Atlanta Compromise Speech. Washington urged Blacks to seek economic security before political or social equality. In 1973, Atlanta became the first major city in the South to elect an African-American mayor, Maynard H. Jackson.

Dr. Sargent posted an opening for an assistant to the minister at Friendship. The position was reserved for a student. When the announcement came to my attention, I wasn't interested especially because I was apprehensive about my lack of preparedness. Dr. Sargent was God-fearing, very articulate, brilliant, and an excellent preacher and teacher of the Word. I never thought I could be a co-laborer to this pastor who—although was short in stature—was a giant of a man who had served for a time as interim president of ITC.

Mrs. Barbara Arrington, secretary at the Morehouse School of Religion, strongly suggested that I apply for this position. I took her advice, and in April 1986, I received notification that the church had chosen me as the assistant to the minister. I was to start the fourth Sunday in April, serving under Dr. Sargent's direction, and I was accountable to him.

Wow! How could this happen, that a young man from Dolomite, Alabama would be called to serve in a big city with such an influential African-American history and presence? This appointment was unbelievable. My only regret was that my father was not alive to see what he'd told me would unfold in my life. He had passed away from prostate cancer on the Sunday morning of August 25, 1984.

I had no expectations regarding the actual duties and responsibilities of the assistant to the minister. Would I be placed on a rotating schedule with Dr. Sargent for Sunday sermons and services or Bible study? Or would I be creating a new ministry?

To my surprise, Dr. Sargent assigned me to visit at least two nursing homes per week and provide a monthly log of my visits. Also, I had to name the persons I attended to and give a synopsis of my encounters. At the time, I thought that while nursing home visitations were necessary, it was not what I had expected to be a part of my responsibilities at the church.

I learned an invaluable lesson, not only for me but also for so many of the residents because so many of them had no one to visit them. Dr. Sargent knew how valuable this experience would be for my growth and development in ministry and in the church.

Patricia Cranton authored a book titled, Professional Development as Transformative Learnings: New Perspective for Teachers of Adults, (Jossey-Bass Publishers, San Francisco, 1996). As Cranton's title reveals, I am convinced Dr. Sargent knew that self-directed learning would transform my life for ministry.

He also placed me on the board of Christian education at the church and the building committee. I had no role on the building committee but to be present for their meetings. I never had to report to Dr. Sargent anything that happened or that was discussed in the building committee meetings. Since nothing seemed to be required of me, I used to wonder why he had placed me on that committee. What was the purpose?

Dr. Sargent knew my thoughts about the proposed addition; the rendering and the plans were not very impressive. Maybe he knew more than I gave him credit for. Perhaps I was appointed to the building committee to see firsthand the church politics involved with that committee. After serving for two years in the assistant to the minister's capacity and three years later as assistant minister, Dr. Sargent announced his retirement on July 7, 1991, effective August 4, 1991. Dr. Sargent's agreement with the church was that he would have to give the church a thirty-day notice if he decided to leave.

I learned about his retirement at the same time as the rest of the congregation. I had no prior knowledge of his planning to retire as pastor. However, in his announcement, he told the church that they had what they needed already in place. He was referring to me.

I had submitted applications to serve as pastor at other churches and was under consideration at two of them, First Baptist Church in Meridian, Mississippi, and New Shiloh Baptist, in Columbus, Georgia. I had never considered that Friendship might become vacant or that I would be a candidate for the position. How could I succeed someone like Dr. Charles Jackson Sargent?

An Invitation to Destiny

When Dr. Sargent announced his imminent departure, new opportunities became available. My thinking changed. The deacons asked me if I would serve as interim pastor through August. I told them yes without hesitation.

Later, in the week of Dr. Sargent's retirement announcement, I visited the home of Deacon Henry and Deaconess Mamie White. I had visited their home on previous occasions, and they always made me feel welcome. I felt comfortable going to their home. Deacon White gave me this counsel as the interim pastor, "Don't let anyone else preach!" He added, "Let them vote you up or down for the position, but don't let anyone else preach."

Dr. Charles Jackson Sargent

I did as he advised. On Wednesday, September 4, 1991, Friendship Baptist Church of College Park held a called meeting to determine whether they would call me to pastor the church. No other candidates were being considered. I was aware of the meeting, so I decided to spend that day and night in Dolomite to ease some anxiety. The meeting was at 7:00 p.m., and I was both excited about the possibilities and anxious about the outcome.

At approximately 8:30 p.m., while waiting and praying for a positive outcome, I received a telephone call from Jerome Miller, chairman of the deacon board. He announced, "The church has voted to call you as pastor of the Friendship Baptist Church of College Park, Georgia."

I was excited and filled with joy. While on the phone, I tried to keep my composure. I had been serving as interim since August, and now I would function as permanent pastor. This appointment was indeed a fantastic turn of events. Just thirty days after Dr. Sargent's retirement, I had become the pastor at Friendship. I am convinced that the Lord used the five years I served under Dr. Sargent as assistant to the minister and assistant minister to prepare the people to receive a first-time, inexperience clergyman as pastor.

I had gotten to know the people, and the people had gotten to know me. It was apparent that I did not connect to the powers within the church, and I believed that played an essential part in my selection. The people loved Dr. Sargent, but I think those powers within the church had his hands tied. I had observed the relationship between Dr. Sargent and the previous chairman of the deacons, Harry Gibbs. Deacon Gibbs served as chairman before Deacon Miller. He was a younger man who grew up in the church and was the son of a long-time member.

Deacon Gibbs did not seem to be very informed about the universal church and robust policies, but he had grown up during a time when the chairman was in charge; and apparently, he, too, wanted to be in control. He seemed to be uncooperative when it came to working with the pastor. It was evident that he was merely a figurehead for most of the board. Nevertheless, he walked around as if he were the man!

I remembered from Saint John and New Bethlehem in Dolomite, the preacher preached, and the deacons managed and controlled the church's affairs. That same model was in play at Friendship, but you could see that a change was in progress through Dr. Sargent's teaching, structure, and patience. He implemented tenure for the chairman, vice-chairman, secretary of the deacons, trustees, Christian education workers, and ministry leaders. No one could serve in those positions for more than three consecutive years. They would have to rotate out of a leadership position for at least one year.

I do believe Dr. Sargent sought to neutralize the power of the deacon board by involving the trustees. Rather than having a deacon board meeting where all the decisions for the church were made, for the most part, Dr. Sargent would be the only one supporting any position he would take. It was smart of Dr. Sargent to float and support a joint board to include the trustees. Neutralizing the deacon board's power and including others to participate in the church's work and direction—even if inclusion was not his original intent—was the right thing to do.

Dr. Sargent was able to put his structure in place. However, after a while, the trustees' inclusion created tension because both groups wanted to be more powerful. Each desired to weld more influence than the other. Not only that, I saw struggles reminiscent of Jacob and Esau because family members, brothers, and cousins sometimes conflicted. That family conflict spilled over into the church.

One brother was the chairman of the deacons, and the other was the chairman of the trustees, and it was easy to identify a degree of sibling rivalry now in the church. The joint boards moved more progressively, working together. Not only was there diversity of gender and thought, but with others present, the deacons' presentations were more amicable than they were before the boards joined. Many of the deacons changed their tone and behavior when others were in the room with them.

During the first four months of my tenure, things went very well. The worship services, ministry meetings, outreach, financial giving, and other in-house ministries continued as usual, even with a degree of excitement. All the departments served as before, and all worship services were maintained as scheduled with choirs and ushers. There was an uptick in church participation, and offerings increased. It appeared that the church and the new pastor were on their way to a healthy, successful relationship.

I structured a new format for Wednesday night Bible study and started a young adult choir called the Voices of Praise that sang just before Bible study. Several young adult men and women came out of the woodwork, and they had an incredibly right blend of voices. Our Wednesday night Bible study doubled in attendance!

Through the joint boards, we purchased the first drum sets in the church's history. The deacons previously had debated about drums being used during worship and they would never support them. Once placed before the joint boards, the purchasing drums met with approval. This project's success, including drums in our services, created some friction between the two groups. Additionally, because I had requested the drums, no one had wanted to stand against the new pastor.

The church started a pastor's aid group. They were so "in love" with me (smile). I have heard of a "honeymoon" period when churches bring in a new pastor, but I was not familiar with how that worked. It did not take long for me to find out. Without a doubt, the honeymoon phase came to an end.

✝✝✝

SERMON
"What God Has for You It Is for You: Personal Responsibility"

Genesis 37:23–24 (NRSV): *[23]So when Joseph came to his brothers, they stripped him of his robe, the long robe with sleeves that he wore; [24]and they took him and threw him into a pit. The pit was empty; there was no water in it.*

Genesis 37—50 captures the story of Joseph and his dreams and how God brought those dreams to pass despite the hatred and abuse of his brothers. Because God gave Joseph a dream, his brothers hated him for his vision. I believe that this story captures a segment of my ministry at Friendship. I decided to use Genesis 37:19–20 (NRSV) as a springboard for this sermon:

They said to one another, *"Here comes this dreamer. [20]Come now, let us kill him and throw him into one of the pits; then we shall say that a wild beast has devoured him, and we shall see what will become of his dreams."*

What God has for you is for you, but to receive what God has, you must do your part. God is not a genie—just rub your Bible and what you ask is yours for the taking. As believers, you have promised blessings for your life. Every child of God has the destiny to succeed if you do your part. Don't allow obstacles, or hindrances, or apparent failures to discourage you. The promise is still real.

And God has given to every believer, as Second Peter (1:4) tells us, "precious promises." Many of us have learned that in order to receive, often we must go through something to get it. God sometimes allows us to endure challenging trials and tribulations to refine and develop a sense of trust and dependence. Many in the church want God's blessings but do not want to go through anything to receive those blessings. We must learn to accept this truth; sometimes, God allows us to go through things in life to make us better and to help us appreciate God and the blessing more.

God expects all of us to have high expectations for the future. Dreams are essential for future successes. However, one of life's most challenging lessons is that things don't always go the way we plan.

How do you bounce back when your hopes and dreams come crashing down? What should you do to stay focused on that which has not yet manifested?

Joseph's brothers despised his dreams, and they would do what they could to destroy them. His God-given vision was that one day he would be in a position of authority, and they would serve him. An idea sparks the feeling of destiny in your life when tied to your purpose. In this text, we find a dreamer who had to go through a lot to realize his dream. Joseph's dreams revealed his destiny. But it appeared that jealous and hateful brothers would attempt to shatter his dreams. His brothers were willing to kill him because they were jealous of his dreams.

When Dr. Martin Luther King, Jr. gave his famous "I Have A Dream" speech, I wonder if that dream led to his death.

Sometimes it takes courage to share a God-given dream with others. Joseph was a young man when his father Jacob sent him out to check and see if all was well with his brothers tending the flock. When they saw him from afar, they said, "Here comes this dreamer. Come now, let us kill him… and we shall see what will become of his dreams."

But rather than kill him, they sold him to traders who were going to Egypt. Their best efforts could not hinder God's plan for Joseph. At every turn God turned his trials into triumphs. Joseph's story can encourage us to the know that every child of God will succeed. Don't believe the lies about a generational curse—because daddy was a rolling stone, you must be one also; or, because momma was in the streets, I must be there, too. In the life of every believer, God has promised success. Don't get me wrong, you will have failures in your life, but God will use our failures to usher in victories.

Look at some things that led Joseph from a dream to a reality—from a pit to a palace.

First, Joseph dreamed.

If you don't dream, you'll have nothing in life to aim for; a dream serves as direction for your life. We just celebrated fifty years since Dr. King gave his great "I Have a Dream" speech. Today, that speech about a dream still inspires. Joseph dreamed.

Remember the words of Dr. Benjamin Elijah Mays: "It must be borne in mind that the tragedy of life doesn't lie in not reaching your goal. The tragedy lies in having no goal to reach…."

Yogi Berra once said, "If you don't know where you are going, you might wind up someplace else."

A dream predicts your future. Joseph dreamed that he would serve in a position of authority. You don't need to run to Ms. Ann to read your palm or pick up the horoscope every day. All you need is a godly dream. If you don't have a dream for your life, ask God to give you one.

Second, Joseph believed in the dream.

What good is a dream if you don't think that it can be achieved? I know that some dreams seem impossible, but that is the good news about God; with human beings it is impossible, but with God all things are possible. I say all the time that the most crucial thing in life is to believe. Only believe. Jesus said to only believe that you have what you ask for, and you shall receive it.

Third, be faithful where you are.

Joseph dreamed that he would be a man of authority. But he was sold as a slave and then made a housekeeper. He kept the house so well that the master gave him authority over his household affairs. That is why when we are in our jobs; we should work as if we are working for the Lord. Let everything we do, shine! While Joseph was serving in the house, Potiphar's wife lied on him and said he had sought to molest her. They took him to jail.

But look at God! God can allow favor to fall on your life regardless of where you are. One of the reasons some of our dreams don't come to pass is because we are not faithful. Some people say, "When I get that next position, I will show them what I can do." Or "I have a degree in accounting, and they are not going to get anything out of me until I get that position." What you must remember is that Jesus said they that are faithful over a little would become ruler over much. Some of us think that we are above doing some things. But I am a witness that God will give you a raise if you are faithful over a little. Joseph working as a housekeeper and being thrown into prison had nothing to do directly with serving in a position of authority. But he was faithful.

First, Joseph dreamed; he saw his destiny. Second, Joseph believed his dream. Third, Joseph used what he had to the best of his ability and was faithful.

God had a reason for everything that was happening in his life and God has a purpose for everything happening in your life. Just do not abandon the dream! Things might get rough and might not appear to be going as you planned; hang on in there. God is working it out.

The pharaoh had a dream, and none in his court was able to interpret the dream. Then the chief butler remembered how Joseph interpreted dreams while they were in prison. The pharaoh called for Joseph, and when Joseph interpreted the pharaoh's dream, he was promoted.

When a severe famine came, Joseph was in a position to distribute the grain and negotiate sales. When his brothers came to buy grain because of the famine, they did not recognize Joseph. But when Joseph revealed himself to them, he said, *"...You meant evil against me; but God meant it for good..."* Genesis 50:20 (NKJV).

Joseph aiding his brothers is a messianic model. For Joseph to save his brothers, family, and a nation, he had to suffer. He had to go through everything he went through to arrive at the point of having authority over Egypt. Look at what Jesus had to go through to deliver us! Who would have ever thought that the world would be calling upon the name of a peasant born in a stable?

Who would have thought that the Son of God would come into the world like that? But God had ordained it before the foundations of the world. Believe me when I tell you, regardless of what things are looking like around you or what you must go through, what God has for you is for you!

Claim it and receive it in the name of Jesus!

A bit of wisdom often attributed to Abraham Lincoln is, "Success is not letting dead ends kill you." God would not allow death to kill Jesus. The cross was not a dead end; it was there that God took the negative and birthed the positive. God allowed His Son to die while making all believers alive in God. Jesus died so that we might live eternally. Amen!

✝✝✝

When my tenure began as pastor at Friendship, the congregation was planning an addition to the existing structure to increase worship and educational space. I noticed there appeared to be extraordinarily little excitement or interest in this project among the membership. Something about this project just was not right. Later I found out that the contractors were working too closely with some committee members. What was evident to me was that the people in the church were going along to get along, blindly following committee members for this project.

Additionally, financial giving to this project was not at a level to support the desired outcome, and it appeared that Dr. Sargent had little input, if any, before he retired. The church building sat on approximately one acre of land with four small areas around the church for parking. The church could seat about three hundred in the sanctuary, and Dr. Sargent had led the church to add wings on both sides of the sanctuary in 1985, adding another two hundred and twenty seats and twenty-five new parking spaces across the street.

The sanctuary expansion was barely a year old before it became apparent that the addition would not accommodate the current level of congregational growth. In 1986, Dr. Sargent established another building committee chaired by John W. Cox, a man held in high regard by many members of the church. He was homegrown. The residents of College Park, the African-American community, and some Whites throughout the metropolitan Atlanta area recognized him as a mover and shaker in the region. Mr. Cox was a vice-president at Delta Airlines and sat on several boards, including the Martin Luther King, Jr. Center for Non-Violent Social Change. He had close ties to Mrs. Coretta Scott King, Mayor Andrew Young, Mr. Jessie Hill, Mr. John Ward, Mrs. Juanita Abernathy, and other influential people in the Atlanta area.

A rendering of the future church building that Mr. Cox and the committee had authorized architects to provide was displayed prominently in the vestibule. The rendering showed the existing building with a huge structure attached to the east side. The addition would eliminate the existing parking spaces on that side, and the new sanctuary would seat approximately a thousand people. At the time, attendance was around 700 to 800 each Sunday.

Friendship was known as "the" African-American church in College Park. The church had many educators on all levels—college professors with PhDs, principals, business executives, entrepreneurs—as well as members on boards throughout the region, and politicians. Michael Hightower was the only African-American councilman in College Park, and his brother Anthony was a state legislator. They grew up in Friendship. The Coxes, Hightowers, Prices, Jordans, and Williams, were prominent families in the church. The base of the church was family, and God had placed a young man from Dolomite, Alabama, whose background was not comprised of a list of who's who as their leader. Much like Moses, I felt that I did not have the adequate tools to lead such a people. But also like Moses, I had the assurance of God's presence. I drew on two tendencies I had noticed among African-American congregations when they undertook a building project.

First, the plans were too small to meet the needs for future growth. I had noticed that when congregations entered their new church building, too often there was not enough seating available for all in attendance. Friendship is an excellent example: two wings were added in 1985, and now a new building committee was being formed in 1986.

Second, I had noticed most churches did not plan for adequate parking. Friendship is a prime example of that mistake made by African-American churches when expanding their worship facility. We did not have the landmass to meet the needs of a growing ministry. Therefore, after receiving God's vision and talking with God, I concluded that Friendship had to move to a place with more land.

I have heard seasoned preachers say when a new pastor comes to a church, the last thing they should do is to change anything immediately. But God had given me a vision, and the need was unfolding before my eyes. I did not see myself as doing anything new or different; but rather, I was following the leading of the Holy Spirit. And what helped me was that God threw in the practical component. It was not difficult to see that the church's proposal to add to the existing building was not realistic.

One concern was that the current plan would not allow space for adequate parking. The other issue was that the City of Atlanta was buying property in the immediate area for airport expansion purposes. Nevertheless, a stubborn and litigious few in the church tried extremely hard to convince the congregation that we needed to build on the present site.

Chapter Four

A New Vision

Rendering of the New Facility

I had heard from God, who gave me a dream and a vision that was so real that I committed to embracing it. God led me to Jeremiah 1:5–10 to confirm the Word to me. Jeremiah, like Moses, made excuses not to heed God's call. God responded to Jeremiah, "before I formed you in the womb I knew you."

In other words, I'm sure God was telling Jeremiah something like, "I don't need a lecture from you!" God told Jeremiah to go and speak what the Lord has said, *"See, I have appointed you today over nations and kingdoms to uproot and tear down, to destroy and demolish, to build and plant"* Jeremiah 1:10 (CSB).

Serving with Dr. Sargent allowed me to see things, and God showed me that there were people in positions being used to hinder the church's growth. They were people of power and influence in the church. Like so many in our society, people in the church did not want to lose their "power." Dr. Sargent was not a fighter, and if he had been, I am not sure that he was able to fight. I will always believe that they had him between a rock and a hard place in his desire to expand.

In February 1992, I preached a sermon titled, "Vision." In that message I announced that God had given me a vision, and I put forth everything God had shown me. The church needed to change its direction to meet people's needs, today and in the days to come. It was a comprehensive vision, and for sure, what God showed me could not happen at the present location. On that Sunday, as soon as I said, "God has given me a vision," it appeared that the Devil woke up! Although I felt that I did not have to say it in that sermon, I said it anyway: "We have to move!"

I shared the vision that God had given me. We needed at least fifty to one hundred acres of land so that we could "build ministries that build people."

We were landlocked and needed to move from a depressed area. Because of the Atlanta Airport's growth, people were moving out, and others sold their property. No one was moving into this area. Friendship used to be a church located in the heart of a thriving African-American community, but that was no longer true. The church was supported primarily by those who lived within a half-mile radius, and many members lived within walking distance. The surrounding community was losing residents due to airport expansion and city investments. When Dr. Sargent came to the church, he had laid out a plan for church growth. He gave structure to the church in terms of organization and management, and he added wings to the church, but the vision was still too small. People were now coming to Friendship from all over South Fulton County and beyond. Airport and other business employees in the area found that Friendship was the church for them.

Dr. Sargent had added an 8:15 a.m. service to accommodate airport employees who worked the night shift. That initial service became a favorite of airport workers, but almost 50 percent of other worshipers preferred the earlier service as well. Friendship was certainly in need of a larger facility, and the current location was a problem.

✝✝✝

SERMON
"Vision"

Proverbs 29:18 (KJV): Where there is no vision, the people perish: but he that keepeth the law, happy is he.

My brothers and sisters in Christ Jesus, I am excited to share with you the vision that the Lord has given me regarding the Friendship Baptist Church, and God has confirmed that vision in a dream. I have never been as convinced of God's presence and guidance as I am in our coming together to develop an entire ministry in the name of the Lord.

For the past three and a half years, we have talked about and made plans to build a new church edifice. I have never been as clear as I am today in my understanding of why that building was not erected or at least in a construction phase. The Lord has shown me a wonderful ministry that is ours if we would only claim it. We must look beyond doing business as usual. We must include many ministries that many of our churches (Friendship in particular) are not providing. We are offering, in many instances, less to its people than our churches did decades ago.

The Lord has opened my eyes to a ministry that is ours. This is a ministry that will meet people's needs and a church that would impact the deplorable conditions in which our people find themselves.

Friendship is blessed to have the kind of talented people we have in our church. Tragically, we don't have space or the facilities for so many of them to use their gifts and talents.

My brothers and sisters, we need to move!

We need to move to a location where there are people and more land. The vision that the Lord has given me suggests that we look to purchase fifty to one-hundred acres. We cannot continue to do business as usual regarding Christ's church. Even though we cannot build on all this land at one time, it will offer opportunities for the future.

For approximately the same amount of money that we would spend on an addition at this location, we can purchase land and build a beautiful 2000-seat sanctuary. And by building in a growth area, our membership will triple in a relatively short time. It will triple because we will offer ministries to meet the needs of people. We would have a chapel and several large rooms that would allow us to have three or four significant events happening simultaneously. We would have a multipurpose facility that would house a gymnasium, commercial kitchen, classrooms, a stage for live productions, a banquet room, and a fellowship hall. Then, we would have an educational wing that would lend itself to church school classes, a daycare facility, after-school programs, and an academy. We could have these facilities and not use more than ten acres.

Also included would be a sports complex for our people. With land, you can do a lot of inexpensive things. We would have tennis courts, a ball field, track, and a weight facility in that sports complex. These are facilities that we use daily. If we don't, we should use them so that our bodies will be fit to do the work of Christ.

I can't think of a safer place to come together than in a church community. That's what God has shown me—not just a church building, but a Christian community. We must always care for those who cared for us. I have a deep concern for our elderly, and we have already started new ministries for them. With this kind of church, we can build a high-rise apartment building for our elderly. People can feel safe and establish better relationships with one another.

My brothers and sisters, with this kind of complex, we could have a credit union. Believe it or not, we have a lot of money, and a community like this would nurture the kind of communal support that our people need. Just look at the opportunities! There would be no reason why we can't have an area designated as a health clinic. We have enough doctors and nurses in this church to operate a small hospital. This complex would allow us to establish a counseling center to meet the needs of persons in crisis.

There is no reason why we cannot be in this complex within a year and a half from this date. There is no excuse. We have the money and we have the people. God has blessed us, but if we continue to hoard cash that God has given us for ministry, that same money will burn our souls. Just look at what God is doing! God has blessed Friendship once again to be a leader in modeling ministry. We will not do business as usual. Our brothers and sisters worldwide need to know that no longer can we do ministry with just a place to come on Wednesdays and Sundays.

We need to establish the kinds of ministries found in that first-century church. The Bible tells us that they all came together in one place. They sold all their belongings, and everyone had what they needed, young and old alike. We can build a community. And if by chance, we don't use all the land before we die, at least our children's children will say that we had the foresight. We thought about them.

I am excited because the Lord has shown this to me, and I know that we will have it. It seems like God has put everything in place to help us along. The real estate market is depressed. The land is as cheap as we have seen in decades. The cost of material and labor is at an all-time low. Everything is right for us to move, and we need to move now! There is no need to debate the issue. God has made it possible, and now all we need is to just do it. We don't need to react to what is happening around us; we need to be proactive. We should not wait until the city, state, or federal government tells us we must move from this site. We need to move because God has said so. Our leader is the guidance of the Holy Spirit and not George Bush or Zell Miller. As God speaks to us, we need to hear from heaven. Friendship is building a ministry that enriches people's lives. That's what God wants. That's what God has revealed.

How will we pay for this beautiful and practical community? We are blessed to have assets, but we will go all the way with God through tithes and offerings. We will do it God's way. I believe God for this ministry. I don't see why we cannot burn the mortgage for this ministry within one year of moving into it. God is on our side; we need a community ministry. The church can no longer offer space for worship services, Bible study, and church school only.

We are dying every day. But with a ministry like this in place, we can train our people. We can employ our people. We can love our people and offer nurture for the total person. Let us not forget how we got here. None of us has anything to boast about today. It is not because we are so smart, because we are not. Nor is it because of the sacrifices our forebears made. We are here and have what we have because one Friday evening, soldiers marched a man named Jesus to a hill called Calvary. On that hill, they crucified him. He suffered bled and died so that you and I might have life. More than that, He died so that we might have life more abundantly. He died, not because he had done anything wrong; He was a perfect man. He died because of my sins and your sins. Today, I stand in humble submission, thanking God for Friday. Because I have come to know that without Friday, Sunday morning would not have been possible. It was on Sunday that God raised Him with all authority in his hand. And I can hear Him say, *"And when I am lifted up from the earth, I will draw everyone to myself"* John 12:32 (NLT).

At Friendship, we are going to lift the name of Jesus. We will serve as a testimony to what God can do. I am excited because I know…Yes! I know that God will never leave nor forsake us. If we follow the Holy Spirit's direction, God will give us the desires of our hearts.

I want to share one more thing with you. Jesus had a vision; that is how Jesus was able to do great things. God will not allow a godly vision to go unrealized. Jesus had a dream, although there were those around who could not see His vision. He was committed to the vision that God gave Him. Jesus looked down through the annals of time and could see how His life would save millions upon millions. He had a vision.

Amen!

✞✞✞

Within the next few weeks, I strategized with God and formed a new building committee, confirming one by one without meeting with them together. Before announcing that move, I called Mr. John Cox in for a meeting, knowing that he was not in favor of the change. I allowed him to resign as building committee chairman, which he did immediately. He told me that I was the pastor and that he would support my decision. I could not afford the word getting out that the new pastor has removed Brother John from the building committee.

What I did not expect, however, was the fallout from the idea of moving the church. I thought that John Cox resigning from the building committee would influence family members and friends to embrace the vision of the new pastor. But I was wrong. Without a doubt, I was sure that the word I got came from God. I knew it would not be popular with some, but I felt that the majority would favor the move. I would estimate that at least 75 percent of the members were in favor of the action, or at least were willing to go along with the plan. But of that number, 10–15 percent were diehards who simply would not budge.

I believed that because the church's demographics had changed, and the conversations I heard among the membership, the people were ready to move! No longer were the original families in the majority, although they were still in charge of the church's politics. Most of the church did not like being influenced in this way. But I did not recognize the 10–15 percent's passion for keeping the church in its present location or for standing against what I saw as progress. Regardless, I was on a mission from God, and there was no doubt that we were following God's plan!

The Lord moved me to present my ideas to those with whom I had a relationship in leadership. Deacons Jerome Miller, Larry Younginer, and Howard Green were sounding boards for me. I floated the possibility of including the board of Christian education in the joint boards. I floated this idea because that ministry was the umbrella for all the ministries of the church. This model would relieve some of the tension between the deacons and trustees and would involve members of the board of Christian education in making decisions.

No longer would I be in the middle of two brothers going after each other. No longer would it be the practice for the preacher, deacons, and trustees to make decisions in a back room and leave out a ministry that encompassed every other ministry of the church. No longer would brothers and other family members bring their family conflict to the church (and other members not know it). With the inclusion of the board of Christian education to the joint board, I thought I would have more support for the things God was revealing to me. I felt like Jesus: it seemed like everywhere I went, and everything I offered was not without conflict.

I am convinced, as was with Jesus, when people hear about something new and different, they are hesitant to embrace it. When Jesus entered the synagogue and healed a man with a deformed hand (Matthew 12:10), the people may have thought, "What is this? Stepping out on this level of faith is something we have never seen before!"

The vision God gave me was before its time in the small town of College Park, Georgia. Usually, when people talked about building a new church, for the most part, they were referring to a four to eight hundred-seat sanctuary and a fellowship hall.

For this community to envision one hundred acres of land and a facility with over 80,000 square feet of ministry space to meet the total person's needs was beyond realization. God instructed me to share this vision with the people and lead them to accept the fact that God had promised it, and they would receive it.

Several people have called me a visionary. I have two perspectives of a visionary: 1. A visionary is like a prophet in that if a vision is cast and it does not come to manifestation, then it was not a vision from God. 2. A godly vision will outlive the visionary.

I never doubted that God had given me this vision. Although I had stood on the sidelines and observed other pastors, I never thought that I brought the gifts and talents to ministry that they did. What I have learned and still fully embrace is that I can only use what God has given me. Demonstrating faith in God was all I needed. I have learned that God is seeking a willing spirit and will use everything that God places in you.

The vision God gave me had not been presented to the church before. God gave me a new vision.

The former location of Friendship Baptist Church

Chapter Five

Faith Versus Conflict

Hebrews 11:1–3 (RSV): Now faith is the assurance of things hoped for, the conviction of things not seen. ²For by it the men of old received divine approval. ³By faith we understand that the world was created by the word of God so that what is seen was made of things which do not appear.

Although there was a substantial majority of the congregation in favor of moving the church building from its present location, the fight and passion of the minority were so intense that they became disruptive in Sunday services. One of the prominent mothers of the church pulled me aside one Sunday and said, "My mother put bricks on this church, and we are not going anywhere!"

Although John Cox had resigned from the building committee, he had not resigned from the church. He still had tremendous influence, and I was able to see that impact in a small minority within the church. I believed the majority was embracing the vision God had given me, but they were not very vocal and were not "fighters" like some of those with the minority. I felt just like David going up against Goliath; he was outmatched in every way but one—the presence of God (1 Samuel 17:45).

I asked Mrs. Dorothy Smith, a very energetic and determined lady if she would serve as co-chairperson of the building committee, along with Deacon Larry Younginer.

She responded positively, and I sensed her excitement and enthusiasm. Several things were working to move the vision forward with this appointment. Mrs. Smith was the wife of our music director. She had three children in the church, one with the young adults, one in the youth ministry, and one in the children's ministry. Also, she served as the youth leader. I thought she brought even more momentum to our cause. I had observed how effectively she managed the youth ministry and her relationship with our youth and children participants' parents. Our youth ministries had over 150 youth and children actively participating. I also observed her support of the youth and children's choirs.

Deacon Younginer was the deacons' chairman—well respected, conservative, and an executive with the Coca-Cola Company. He was married with two children involved in our youth ministry. I had a great combination to lead the building committee. These two leaders were well known and respected by the people of the church.

The new building committee had four of the twenty-seven members from the original committee, and I selected four new members to serve with them. When there were twenty-seven members on the building committee with John Cox as chairman, only a handful participated in the decision-making process. With a new committee in place, I thought we were on track to realizing the vision God had given me.

The committee's first assignment was to locate fifty to one hundred acres of land to build our new facility. After a few weeks of searching, the committee found fifty-two acres approximately five miles west of the existing sanctuary. I thought this news from the committee would encourage some of those who were not supportive of the move to reconsider since the proposed site was not far from the present location.

While it may have influenced some, there were still others who were not impressed. When the proposed property was presented to the congregation in a church meeting, the church conference approved it.

I visited the site, located on Old Fairburn Road; however, the land did not have the frontage I thought we needed. But what was more important was that the people were excited about the prospect of moving. There were fourteen acres with a residence adjacent to the fifty-two-acre property. I believed if it could be purchased as well, it would provide the frontage on Old Fairburn Road we needed.

It appeared that everything was falling into place. Still, it was not yet apparent just how vicious the opposition would be nor the degree of legal maneuvering they were willing to employ to stop the project. On April 6, 1992, Dorothy Smith received a letter from a contractor stating that they had a contract with the church to build on the present site. If we were moving in another direction, the contractor wanted compensation for anticipated losses.

There was a tractor that had been sitting at the edge of the church's property for months. I never saw it move and never heard anyone say anything about it being there. It had no significance to any of the leaders of the church. No one had given any thought to a contract. I had sat in on several building committee meetings, and discussions seldom focused on expanding the existing structure in tangible ways. I did learn later that there was a relationship between the building committee chair and the contractor.

On May 10, 1993, there was a called meeting to address the contractor's issue. In that meeting, when the idea of hiring an attorney came up, John Cox made a motion to hire an outside attorney only if the problem was unresolved within two weeks.

Frances Elder, a pastor's aid committee member, made a motion that Pastor Bryant, Deacon Price, and Attorney Bobby Simons resign. The motion failed. That was the first call for an end to my tenure in a church meeting. At the meeting, it was revealed that a few insiders knew about the contractor's contract but never said anything about it previously.

At a meeting on August 13, 1993, a reading from church minutes revealed that Dr. Sargent's name, rather than Pastor Bryant's, was listed as the authorized member who signed the contract. In that meeting, Dorothy Smith resigned as co-chair of the building committee because she felt she was in a "set-up-to-fail" type situation with the contractor's revelation. Dorothy's resignation as the building committee co-chair seemed to prompt second thoughts from the congregation. Since I was the pastor, I had to respond to her resignation. I did not think that her resignation jeopardized the project because, without a doubt, my faith in God did not waver.

By this time, I was thinking that if only others had been present when God gave me the vision of a new site and a dream of a beautiful campus to house ministries on church-owned property; if they could only have been there to hear the birds and to see the people moving around through the Friendship Community Church campus, they would never have doubted that God would work it out.

Nothing could stop the church from moving forward and claiming what God had for us. I saw it! I can share with the people of the Church universal that with God on your side nothing shall be impossible.

This experience taught me that although people can be well-intentioned, I could never fully trust anyone other than God. Also, it was especially noteworthy that a pastor's aid committee member was among those who called for an end to my tenure. They used to tell me that they loved me all the time, so much so that it became annoying.

I often tell the story that I never heard my father tell me, "I love you." I am certain that the culture and exposure to others in an oppressed environment had everything to do with how he communicated with us. I believe that he was more concerned about showing love toward us rather than saying, "I love you." The culture could have suggested that that kind of language was not very "manly" in the African-American community.

But I saw him go to work every day and sometimes work overtime for days at a time. He never allowed us to go hungry or without a roof over our heads. We were never naked, and we never saw him abuse our mother. Cursing was commonplace among people in the community, but I never heard my father use profanity throughout his life. He showed his love for his family through his actions, but never told me, "I love you" with words.

To this day, I am not impressed by people saying to me, "I love you," because I have learned from my father's example that actions speak so much louder than words. There are some things that God never said to me, but I know what God had shown me.

The people wanted to see how I would respond to Dorothy's resignation. I thought Dorothy would stay with the building committee, but she did not survive. After she resigned from the committee, I immediately moved to identify someone else to serve in that position that had the congregation's confidence, energy, and desire to serve in that capacity. I asked Louis Bell, a Trustee of the Church, and a Delta Airlines pilot.

One thing I am known for is not allowing grass to grow under my feet. It was apparent that regardless of what happened in my ministry, God would always be there. Getting things done was at the forefront of my mind. I never wanted people to praise me; I was on a mission from God. And with God, I knew I would not fail. The writer James says, "Faith without works is dead!"

In a meeting on August 13, 1993, Deacon Willie Smith moved that a vote regarding the pastor's tenure be held in thirty days. Ms. Betty Toland, the former church secretary, seconded that motion. The motion carried by sixty to twenty-two.

In that August 13 meeting, Deacon Jerome Miller presented a document dated August 7, 1990. Anthony Hightower had sent the architect a letter that suggested the church did have some legal responsibility in the contractor's situation. The meeting had started at 7:55 p.m. and adjourned at 12:05 a.m. The opposition raised so many issues during that meeting. They appeared to use every tool in their toolbox. It was almost like I was playing quarterback on a football team again. Everyone on the defensive side of the ball comes after you from every direction, and sometimes to escape you must improvise. But I did not have to improvise. All I had to do was remain faithful to God and watch God work to accomplish the purposes of God.

Finally, my opposition got their wish. The church scheduled a meeting to vote on my tenure on September 19, 1993. They chose to vote by secret ballot whether I was to be retained as pastor. Thank God, most people saw no fault in my leadership, and the outcome of the vote to retain the pastor was 422 to 186. The result was a blessing for me and a disappointment to the opposition, but it was not news to God.

Chapter Five

Fighting Back

As pastor, it was imperative that the congregation not see me fight the opposition as if the Lord was not leading me. These people had established relationships with one another on one level or another. One person told me the people watched me to see how I treated my perceived enemies; they thought I would treat them the same way they treated me.

We ended up in court because the opposition filed a restraining order against me. In the ongoing litigation process, the Plaintiffs would change as the various cases continued. Some would drop off while others would sign-on. Some of the people who were with me initially turned against me later in the process. I did not understand some of them going against me; nothing had changed, and I had not done anything wrong.

Why were people fighting me?

I remember reading Numbers 16 time after time during our struggles, and what stood out to me in that narrative was that the people wanted to be equal with Moses. Korah, Dathan, and Abiram were leaders of two-hundred and fifty men who challenged Moses' and Aaron's authority by rejecting God's order. I never thought that I carried myself or managed the church as if I were untouchable. Nothing could be further from the truth. What was it about me that kept the fights going?

Allegedly, I was arrogant. I never thought of myself in this way, but most people do not see the traits within themselves that turn people away. One thing I do know, I had a ton of confidence in the Lord. But the more I pondered these issues, the clearer it became. The people who came against me may have regarded themselves as being upstanding in the community and, for sure, more so than this preacher from Dolomite.

All of them were college graduates. Some held top management positions with major corporations, some were business owners, members of the political community, and activists. For the most part, they approached life from an empirical view—what we can prove—and not from a faith perspective. They were smart, but just as the Lord told Jeremiah, I was not intimidated, nor was I afraid of their faces. I was on a mission from God, believing every word God gave me, and I was constantly reminded by the Lord, "I am with you."

So maybe my opposers had a "Korah" spirit and were unwilling to accept me in the pastor's position, leading the Friendship people. But I also realized how important it was to have allies by my side whom the people knew and believed. I did not think that God would have me out there by myself; but I also knew that God could have chosen not to involve any other people, and everything still would have been alright.

Along the way, I found that God was using different people during the testing and developing to support and stand with me. Although some stood with me at one time, they turned and joined with the plaintiffs. Even though they did not get along with each other, they came together to oppose my vision for the church.

After that episode, it would not be long before another crisis hit Friendship. On Sunday, June 26, 1994, I received a call from Deacon William Howard Green, Sr., vice-chairman of the deacon board and finance chairman. At the time, the deacon board vice-chairman automatically served as finance chairman, regardless of his qualifications. However, Deacon Green was budget director for the Centers for Disease Control and Prevention (CDC), and was not uninformed regarding finance. He told me, "They've locked the church," and he could not get inside.

I had heard of people locking out the preacher but had never heard of people locking everyone out. I lived less than five miles from the church, so it did not take me long to get there. When I arrived, it was apparent that the door locks had not been changed, but rather, compromised. Deacon Green crawled through a small window on the east side of the building and opened all the doors to the sanctuary.

The 8:15 a.m. service did not start as scheduled. Slowly, the people were standing outside of the building started to come inside. Others were troubled by what had taken place and decided not to stay. Some just milled about outside and met the 11:00 a.m. worshippers as they entered.

Once inside, we tried to have some semblance of a worship service, but the opposition had lined the walls of the sanctuary and had begun to sing, "We Shall Overcome!" They would not allow the service to move forward, so I asked that we pray instead of trying to conduct a traditional worship service. I did not think that prayer would be interrupted, and it was not.

After a few people prayed, we dismissed and left the church. In no time, news about the problems at Friendship spread throughout the community. It was indeed an embarrassment for the church that had stood as a pillar in the city. The actions of the opposition that day were a genuine disappointment for the Universal Church.

A couple of Sundays later, John Williams, an incredibly quiet and soft-spoken trustee, after service, told me in the presence of others, "I guess they forgot you were a quarterback in school. You got knocked down a lot, but you always had to get back up!"

I had never made that comparison! While it is true that I always got back up as a football player, now it had to do with the Lord's work and the power of God. I knew the power of God; it was nothing within my own ability that empowered me to get back up when the opposition's attacks hit the church. What I knew was, "The battle was not mine; it was the Lord's."

John was not aware that I had committed to God that I would not abandon God in any way! I used to hear people say, "I am so crazy until I believe everything God says." Well, not crazy, but what they were inferring was that their faith in God was so strong that nothing could move them away from God's promises. My faith in God was so strong until God shielded me from any obstacles that would have derailed the vision that God had seeded in me. My faith in God continued to propel me forward as if nothing could stop me.

Early on the morning of October 15, 1993, I was served a subpoena at my home ordering me to be in court at 1:00 p.m. that day. I called Deacon Green and told him about the court summons and that I was not going. After all, how can I be served to be in court within a few hours?

Deacon Green told me that I needed to go and that he would meet me there. He asked if I knew a lawyer who could go with us. I called Pastor A. J. McMichael of Mount Nebo Baptist Church, who had served as Dr. Sargent's teaching assistant at ITC. He referred me to Attorney Ted Lackland.

Attorney Lackland was not available, but he sent his associate, Attorney Karen Fultz, to work with us. Deacon Green and I met at Piccadilly's restaurant down the street from his office at the CDC. We had lunch and then drove to the Fulton County Court House.

It was a good thing that I took Deacon Green's advice because the opposition had aggressively put their plan in place. They requested a restraining order to prohibit me from entering the church the following Sunday. I am sure that if I had not shown up, they would have been able to get the order mandated. They had their attorney in place, and I will always believe that they knew someone within the court system to get a hearing so quickly. I felt like Jesus when He went into a kangaroo court of unauthorized accusers. But I love the omnipresent, omniscient, and omnipotent God who put the right people in the right place at the right time for the church and for me.

Attorney Fultz was able to argue our case for a postponement of the order until we could gather more information and that I could preach on Sunday, much to the displeasure of the opposition.

That was our first court date. I never could have believed that we were nowhere near the end. We were in court on and off from October 15, 1993 to March 18, 2003.

One might ask, "Why would you go through this turmoil?"

Several preachers asked me, "Why don't you just leave those folks?"

The simple answer is that I was on a mission from God.

Despite the litigation, Friendship flourished during those ten years. We were able to add twenty new ministries and 2,100 people joined the church. Also, we were able to make substantive changes in our constitution and bylaws that the courts had exposed as vulnerabilities. By doing so, we were guarding ourselves against this kind of future disruptions.

We had to plan and strategize our efforts to fight off the opposition's legal maneuvering, and I found it necessary to let the people in the church know that there were others with me. There was no greater influential voice than the chairman of the deacons, Larry Younginer. The opposition sought to settle the dispute by sending our lawyer conditions to resolve all issues. We had heard that from them before, but this time they spelled out the terms. I think that the response from Larry Younginer is worth noting here because we concluded that the opposition's request for a settlement was unrealistic.

Their rationale for settlement was based on two assumptions:

First, they believed that since the last vote on the pastor's tenure was 447 to 322 to retain the pastor, that indicated the church was evenly split and there was no hope for healing the rift.

Second, arbitration could not determine fraud and deceit; the arbitrator's decision is not binding and, therefore, appealable. The parties' entrenched position made anything less than the separation of the present minister from the church unacceptable to them.

Opposition Proposal for Settlement:

1. The group desiring to leave continues with its relocation efforts, with a date-specific for relocation. The present minister and those who want to leave Friendship Baptist Church on Harvard Avenue in College Park may do so with the blessing of those who remain.

2. The members who leave and relocate will receive the deed to the newly purchased property. Interest in the plans for the church's construction will transfer to the members of the new church. The Friendship Baptist Church of College Park will retain all the College Park property.

3. All funds (liquid assets) of the church, including the building funds, will be divided, with 50 percent between the two congregations.

4. The relocating group is responsible for the indebtedness incurred for the new property's improvement. To that end, it may be necessary for the relocating group to incorporate as distinct entity.

5. Until the physical separation occurs, both parties will be permitted to worship as separate entities at Friendship Baptist Church. We propose that services be alternated on an odd-even Sunday basis at 8:00 a.m. and 11:00 a.m.

6. The group which is to relocate may retain the services of the present minister. The Friendship Baptist Church of College Park will engage another or several minister's services to conduct their services and service their spiritual needs.

When I first read their proposal, I thought "There is no way that we would agree to these conditions." The congregation had expressed their desire to retain me as pastor on three separate occasions. Most of the members had given their approval to move to the new location.

God gave me the confidence I needed not to agree to their proposal. There was no doubt in my mind that God had placed me there, and only God could remove me. I was on a mission from God!

I had a conversation with the chairman of deacons and the attorney, and we constructed a letter in response to their proposal. Our response was first presented in a deacon's meeting before being presented to the church conference by Deacon Larry Younginer.

We were fighting back!

"As chairman of the board of deacons of the Friendship Baptist Church, I am making this report to the members of the church in its duly scheduled church conference of August 28, 1994. The information submitted in this report results from the board of deacons' actions in one or more regularly scheduled board meetings. The deacons have thoroughly discussed all the activities in this report in a regularly scheduled board meeting. Wherever there were actions that required a vote of the board, the vote was unanimous. This report represents the will of the majority of the board of deacons of the Friendship Baptist Church.

"The board of deacons believes the plaintiffs were without merit, out of order, against the majority's will. The plaintiffs have demonstrated a refusal to accept the rulings of the courts of this county and state. Furthermore, the plaintiffs and those who support them are fully aware that their actions are in opposition to the Holy Scriptures and God's will.

"The board of deacons concluded based on a history of public and private events, spanning more than a year in this church's life. For instance, you, the members of this church, have voted on the tenure of Reverend Bryant on three separate occasions.

Specifically:

"You overwhelmingly voted for Reverend Bryant for his initial call to the pastorate of this church.

"Deacon Willie Smith issued a call for a vote on the pastor's tenure during an August 13, 1993 business meeting of the church. The election took place on September 19, 1993, and the members of this church again confirmed the pastor's tenure.

"The judge ordered a vote on all the officers of the church, including the pastor. The election took place on January 23, 1994, and for the third time, you voted to retain Reverend Bryant as your pastor.

"On every occasion, you have demonstrated your support of Reverend Bryant as the pastor of this church. Our church covenant, by which we govern ourselves, clearly states that we will cheerfully recognize the majority's right to govern. The majority rule has no meaning to the plaintiffs.

"We have felt forced to defend ourselves in the court systems before five judges and an arbitration panel. They have used three different attorneys to file numerous charges and claims against the pastor and former chairman of the board.

More specifically:

- The pastor and former chairman were charged with fraud and deceit. Two independent investigations turned up no proof of wrongdoing.

- The pastor was charged with mismanagement of funds. Neither the pastor nor the board chairman sign or issue checks or handle any of the church funds in any way.

"In every instance, the courts have ruled against the plaintiffs' requests and in favor of the defense. The plaintiffs did not receive a single victory in the court system, and yet in the face of legal setback after legal setback, they have vowed to keep up the fight.

"These are the recommendations from the Board of Deacons in response to the settlement offer from the Plaintiffs:

- The board of deacons unanimously recommends denying the request to split the assets of the church.

- The church sent a resolution to the court requesting a summary dismissal of all the court actions submitted by the plaintiffs.

- That Deacons Harry Gibbs, Walter Rainey, and Richard Summerall, although silenced, be removed entirely from the board of deacons.

- A request to remove trustees Will Grimes, Ted Price, and Milton Tucker from the board of trustees. [A unanimous vote removed these men from the board of Trustees.]

- That plaintiffs must be expelled from the church."

To illustrate just how complex church politics can be, these are the words of the chairman of the deacons who fully participated with me and the attorney in drafting this response to the plaintiffs. This recitation from Deacon Younginer was a powerful position statement. However, Younginer later would join the plaintiffs.

What changed? Why would Deacon Larry Younginer join with persons that he had defended himself against outrageous charges? I was acutely aware that there were a significant number of people who believed in me and what I had told them that the Lord told me. They relied on me to stay firm, and I could see the amazement in people that I could stand against what appeared to be such strong personalities. Some told me that they could not do what I was doing. That was clear to me because God had not called them to be me. Some people trusted every word that came from my mouth. I believe that faith in God moved many of them; while others, not wanting to be embarrassed or experience failure, motivated others. Whatever their reason, God had them there for me.

I saw the tension every day. Specifically, every Sunday I saw the uneasiness that was upon so many of the people. Some people used to be best friends had now become, at best, as strangers—not speaking to one another. But most vital during it all, I still had the faith that could move mountains, and some could see that in me and give God glory.

As I look back, I can see why some said to me, "You are a strong leader," but I resisted. I am slow to accept compliments because I know they are not about me; it is all about God. If you want to give praise for the miraculous things you see in your life, first give God credit, then embrace your blessing.

Throughout my ministry, God has allowed me to make room for other people. As a pastor and leader, I did not have to take up all the oxygen in the room. I consciously endeavored to allow others to use what God had given them to enhance the work of God. This position created a real dichotomy: I have always experienced others whom I thought were more gifted, but I never gave them a place above me. From my dad, I learned never to look down on anyone; while at the same time, never allow anyone to look down upon you.

There was never a question of whether we would see the vision come to reality. The only question was, "When?" I am sure that others pondered the question as well, but it did not concern me because I knew the answer was based on God's time and not ours.

I had heard how people in some churches acted in ungodly ways the way they treated one another. But I never would have thought that all the sophisticated, intelligent, standard barriers of the community at Friendship would have participated in the disruption of a worship service. When I saw what they had done to stop the church from fulfilling the vision God had given, I remembered the book of Nehemiah and went back to reread it for encouragement.

Although things were happening to distract me, the Lord kept my focus. I turned to Nehemiah 4:1 and following passages, where Sanballat, Tobiah, the Arabs, Ammonites, and Ashdodites heard that the repair to Jerusalem's walls was progressing and the gaps were being closed, and they became furious. I saw some of that attitude among those who were not in favor of building in the new location. They became angry, and some even displayed an attitude of hatefulness. It was not hard to see that the project was moving forward, and I prayed fervently that God would continue to lead, guide, and protect us.

I could not believe what was taking place at Friendship! The experience brought me to the realization that the opposition was willing to do anything to stop me and this project. God had given me a vision and instructions to move forward, along with the promise that God's presence would be with me. One of the church mothers told me, "You have to be a man of faith because you could not do what you are doing without faith in God!" She was exactly right because I was constantly reminding myself where I came from and from where the Lord had brought me.

God had proven to be faithful, and if God did nothing else for me or my ministry, God already had done enough. I can see now what my mother was thinking when she said, "Donald Earl, I want you to be a good Christian, but I don't want you to be a preacher!" She knew that church folks can be extremely destructive, much like a tornado destroying everything in its path.

Like Nehemiah, I could not stop the work that God had given us because God never promised me that we would not have obstacles, trouble, or disappointment. But God did promise God's presence. I was on a mission from God.

When the building project's opposition leaders filed an injunction to prohibit me from serving as a pastor, it was evident that they were willing to stop the project by any means necessary. But God again assured me the work of the building project would continue. But just as important, the day-to-day operations of the church, administration, Sunday worship services, Bible studies, and pastoral care ministries had to continue. I still needed to prepare sermons and Bible study lessons and make sure that any public comments did not degrade or promote fighting.

I prayed without ceasing, and all through this ordeal, God gave me peace. I was able to rest and sleep at night. God was aware of all that I had to do, and that the people needed to see in me a man of strength who—though soft-spoken—was obedient to God. Many of the members were heartbroken by what was going on, but they continued to come to Bible study and worship services. In those ministries, God gave a word that encouraged all of us to keep running to see what the end would be.

But even worship services and Bible study were not without distractions. When I would stand to preach on Sundays or to teach on Wednesdays, several of them would get up and walk out. But what they did not know was that when they walked out, God strengthened me by saying, "Okay, Donald Earl, you can go on. Teach and preach. I have removed the distracters."

What was affirmed for me after the first court date and any attempt to distract me was that God is faithful. I knew without question that regardless of what happened or what was said, God was in control. I took the same attitude as Nehemiah when his opposers tried to get him to come down, talk with them, and stop working. He responded (Nehemiah 6:3): "So I sent messengers to them, saying, 'I am doing important work and cannot come down. Why should the work cease while I leave it and go down to you?'"

It was apparent to me that in every situation, God was at work for my good. Whenever something happened to hinder the work, I began to look forward to seeing how God would work it out! God is faithful and demonstrated it time and again!

During this time, I used to get nasty, unsigned notes pushed under my door. After reading a couple of them, the Spirit of God led me, from that time on, to pick them up and immediately place them in "file thirteen" if the sender did not identify themselves. I never read anything that was not signed or did not contain an indication of who it was from, so I never got what others intended to disturb my spirit. God protected me.

The Lord strictly commanded me not to fight from the pulpit. God led me to preach about faith and the love of God and not about the divisions. When I went to the pulpit to preach, there were still some detractors sitting in the pews with their arms folded and stern faces, but that did not affect me because God had given me my assignment.

The faithfulness of God is further demonstrated by the fact that even through this period, people were still joining the church. Two weeks never passed without someone uniting with us. It was amazing to see the unwelcoming faces of the opposition when people walked down to join. They did not want to see the church prosper in any way, even if it meant saving a lost soul.

Before all the tension and litigation, we used to have Love Fellowship, a short period during the worship service to greet other worshippers, whether nearby or across the aisle. The opposition turned this wonderful ministry into an opportunity for recruitment and strategy meetings; therefore, we discontinued the Love Fellowship from our services.

My heart goes out to those brave, compassionate souls who hung in there with us during all the strife. I am confident that we grew spiritually, and that was a benefit—growing the number of members at Friendship who simply wanted to serve God and do God's will. And God provided for us. When we were thirsty, God gave us water from a rock; when we got hungry, God fed us manna from heaven. In other words, even during the battle, the Lord provided everything we needed to keep on keeping on. Although there were many setbacks, God continued to give us victories and the faith needed to know that we would win the war. God prospered us!

You may never believe how determined the opposition was to get rid of me, but I was on a mission, and I was not alone. Then God showed me plainly: they were not after me; they were after God. God had given me a vision, and there was no way on my part that I would let God down.

As I mentioned before, from that first court date we were in and out of court for the next ten years. When we defeated one group, another would emerge. Meanwhile, ministry never stopped. As a matter of fact, ministries had increased. More than that, people were attracted to the church and claiming membership. The Friendship people proved to be excellent for God in times of trouble.

On October 15, 1993, Judge Bayneum heard the motion for a temporary restraining order against Pastor Bryant and Deacon James R. Price. Judge Bayneum denied their motion.

On October 22, 1993, a second motion for a temporary restraining order came before Judge Josephine Holmes Cook and an oral motion by the appellants for ratification of an October 8, 1993 conference. Judge Cook denied the appellants' oral motion. She entered a temporary restraining order preventing anyone from disrupting the orderly functions of the church.

You can only imagine what it was like to pastor and encourage the people under these conditions—not only about what was happening in the church but also in their personal lives. I was so impressed with how God used me during these times. Somehow God always put a smile on my face. When I greeted my haters with joy, they became furious. But the Lord had taught me how to love my enemies, and I did not display a foul spirit.

When members were sick, I visited with them. Despite legal battles, I conducted funerals, Wednesday Bible studies, and Sunday worship services. I was able to preach and teach as if the Lord was orchestrating my movements like a puppet. We sent the word out to bless and not to curse. God continued to give me sermons and lessons that could and would benefit every believer.

We held church conferences quarterly, but it seemed as if we had them weekly. If it wasn't a called meeting, it was a joint boards meeting, or deacons' or trustees' meeting. No matter which one it was, for me every meeting was like "Friday Night Fights!"

It seemed like there was never a meeting where the tenure of the pastor did not come up for a vote. I felt like I was in a lions' den. These meetings drove me to pray more sincerely and often. But I could not lose sight of the fact that God had brought me through every situation without fail to remind our parishioners—and me—of the presence and power of God!

✝✝✝

SERMON
"God Is Able"

Daniel 6:19–20 (CEV): At daybreak the king got up and ran to the pit. 20 He was anxious and shouted, "Daniel, you were faithful and served your God. Was he able to save you from the lions?"

The lion is an inhabitant of the open country. A large male is about ten feet long, including the tail, about three feet at the shoulders, and weighs about five hundred pounds. Of all the animals in the creation of God, the lion is called "king of the jungle."

A man is no match for a lion.

During biblical times, lions were used for sport. Men were thrown into arenas to fight lions with only their bare hands. The lions could rip them apart. As a form of capital punishment, men threw other men into pits with hungry carnivorous lions. Some early church believers were fed to lions because they would not worship idol gods or the emperors.

In this Old Testament text, the king ordered Daniel to be thrown into a den of lions. From this text, every child of God should find exceeding strength, comfort, and encouragement to stand firm against impossible odds. Too often, when it appears that the chips are down, we give up on God.

- When our backs are against the wall, we give up on God.

- When we go to the doctor and are told there is nothing else medically that can be done, we give up on God. When they tell us that we have only six months to live, we leave their office with a bowed head, as if to say, "It's over."

- When the mortgage lender tells us that foreclosure is inevitable, or when the banker says that the bank denies our loan, we give up on God.

But I have come to remind us that the God we serve is able! When it comes to the impossible, you can find God on center stage. When we prepare for surgery, and the doctor tells us that there should be no problem, let me tell you that the doctor cannot guarantee success. That doctor cannot heal; for they are merely performing the surgery.

God says, *"For I am the LORD who heals you"* (Exodus 15:26). No psychiatrist can guarantee that you will leave sound and in your right mind after lying on their sofa for twelve months. For God says He will keep your mind in perfect peace. (Isaiah 26:3). No amount of money can guarantee you a life filled with love, peace, and happiness. God says, *"The silver and gold belong to me..."* (Haggai 2:8).

This text can help everyone know that there is a God who can do the impossible! Daniel was one of the young men who was deported to Babylon when King Nebuchadnezzar invaded Jerusalem. As you know, the Babylonians destroyed the Temple, burned the walls, and transported the best and brightest Israel had to offer to Babylon. When Daniel and others arrived in Babylon, it was evident that he was extremely gifted, and because he used his gifts, he was elevated in the Babylonian Empire. Because of Daniel's ascension to power, some were jealous.

Daniel became one of only three presidents in the entire empire. The other presidents wanted to find fault in Daniel. They tried to come up with a plan that would make him lose favor with the king. They could find no problem with his character because

Daniel was a man of integrity, and they knew that he was loyal to his God. They knew that Daniel would not let a day go by without praying to God three times.

In his upper room, there was a window facing Jerusalem, and three times a day, he would bow and offer prayers to God as he faced the direction of the holy city. Those who sought to trap him went to the king. Because they could not find any fault in Daniel, they decided to offer the king a proposal that stated, "If anyone prayed to another god other than the king for thirty days, they would be thrown into a den of lions."

Well, they knew that Daniel prayed to the true and living God, and now they felt like they had him. The king signed the legislation and affixed his seal. They later went to the king and told the king that Daniel was praying to another God. And because the king had signed legislation, he could not go back on his own order. Although he did not want to have Daniel thrown to the lions, he had no choice! The next morning the king ran to the den to see about Daniel.

He hurried and called for Daniel and asked, "Daniel, servant of the living God...has your God, whom you continually serve, been able to rescue you from the lions?"

Daniel responded and said, "May the king live forever. My God sent His angel and shut the lions' mouths; and they haven't harmed me, for I was found innocent before him. And also before you, Your Majesty, I have not done harm."

I want to look at a few things that jumped out of this text that will encourage every believer who finds themselves in impossible situations to trust God!

First, Daniel had a relationship with God.

Daniel shows us that even in a foreign land, he stayed in communication with God. He was in an area where idol worship was commonplace; a place where anything goes. People all around him were not serving God; they were following the king and their selfish desires. They were not concerned about God if they got the house, the car, the job, the man, the woman, the dope, the bling-bling—and later for God.

Daniel had a relationship with God. Daniel was wise because he served God. The psalmist said, "The fool has said in his heart, There is no God" (Psalm 14:1). When we face difficult situations, we need to know that we have a God to call on.

The principle is the same in the world; the buzz word used to be "connections." If you knew someone in a critical position, they might help you in your situation. With God, we have connections. The young children used to say, "I got the hook-up." There is no better hook-up than to be hooked-up with God; therefore, establish a relationship with the Lord!

Second, Daniel was a man of integrity.

Those who sought to trap him could find no fault in him. Not only did Daniel serve God, but he also was faithful in his daily duties. Integrity will take you where money cannot. The Bible tells us that a good name is more valuable than silver and gold. Daniel walked on the right path. He walked in integrity!

I think about our young brother Michael Vick, and my heart goes out to him. I don't know what he did, but you will smell like a hog if you hang around the hog pen. Now I need to say something else about that: just because he may have made a mistake, that is no reason for us to torture him. And some have done a whole lot worse than being accused of fighting dogs.

We ought to position ourselves to support him and others, just like the Jews did King David when he had Uriah killed after committing adultery with his wife. They declare to this very day that he was their greatest king. Though he made a mistake, they did not forget what he had done for them. All last week we heard about Elvis Presley, who has been dead for thirty years. His home brings in more than fifty million dollars a year.

Thousands upon thousands of people file by his house every year. Elvis died a junkie in his bathroom, but the people who love him have not forgotten what he did. It seems like everybody can forgive except our people.

Jason Giambi admitted using steroids, and the commissioner of baseball said, "Okay, there will be no disciplinary actions taken." And he is playing with the Yankees. A mistake is a mistake. When caught, you are caught. How can we help others get their lives back together? But Daniel walked in righteousness, with no proof found against him. Daniel walked blamelessly. And when we walk blameless before the Lord, God is committed to keeping us in divine care.

Third, we see the inability of humanity to solve problems.

We must understand that there is such a thing as human limitation. There are some things that human beings just cannot do. This text is set up in such a way to dispel any idea that a person had anything to do with Daniel's deliverance.

Let me highlight this by sharing examples:

1. The king could not do anything because he had signed the document and sealed it with his signet ring.

2. Daniel was placed in a den with hungry lions.

3. A stone blocked the lion's den's entry and exit so he could not escape. There was no way any human action could have saved Daniel.

These, my brothers and sisters, are times when we face situations that only God can get us out. There's underemployment. You work your fingers to the bone and still cannot get ahead—can't find employment. You're losing your home. You're losing the one you love. Your children are taking a wayward path full steam ahead. A financial breakthrough does not come your way. Your health is declining, and nothing can change its course. You're dealing with recurring sin addictions—sex, drugs, immorality—and there is no hope for change. The lion's den highlights human limitations. How can you mend a broken heart? But God can do exceedingly abundantly above anything we ask or think (Ephesians 3:20).

Fourth, the God we serve can do anything.

When God spoke to Abraham and Sarah and promised them a son in their old age, Abraham was ninety-nine and Sarah was ninety. When Sarah heard that the Lord had promised she and Abe a child in their old age, she laughed. Then God raised the question, "Is there anything too hard for the LORD?" Then God promised to return in a year's time and they would have a son.

Back then, there was no Viagra®, no Levitra®, no cream, and all the other stuff that people put in their bodies. The God we serve is able! You must have faith in God. Daniel had faith because he never stopped praying. God's prescription to increase confidence is: "Know Me better, and you will trust Me more."

The more you know about God, the more you can trust God. Great faith comes by cultivating a relationship with God. Daniel talked with God; he was no stranger to God. Triumph over trials and temptations comes by faith in God.

The king asked Daniel, "Was your God able?"

Daniel could have said, "O king, the proof is in the pudding. I am still here." But he went on to tell the king what God had done. The Lord sent an angel to shut the lions' mouth. Psalm 34:7 (NIV): *"The angel of the Lord encamps around those who fear him, and he delivers them."*

God takes pleasure in life's difficult situations that are impossible for us to increase our faith. That is why God promoted Jesus from the grave to glory, to destroy the last enemy—death.

Note, too, that Jesus had a relationship with God. He was in constant communication. Jesus said, *"I can do nothing of Myself"* John 5:30 (MEV).

Jesus was a man of integrity. He knew no sin, but He became sin for us; and just as we were tempted, He was yet without sin. Fully human and fully God at the tomb of Lazarus, Jesus realized human limitations, so He called on God. Jesus knew that God could and would do the impossible. That is what led Him to Calvary, knowing that God is able!

Amen!

✝✝✝

Although there was a brief period of respite with no outward conflict, the opposition worked every day behind the scenes to weaken the church and destroy me. Although I could not see what was going on, God had clear vision. Not only was God able to see what they were doing and planning, God knew their minds. God knew their hearts. Hiding the contents of the soul from God is not an option.

On December 10, 1993, Judge Frank Hull proposed an election process, and the result of the election would put an end to all litigation. Unfortunately, this attempt at closure fell through as others had done.

In June 1994, I attended the Hampton's Minister's and Choir Guild Conference at Hampton University, in Hampton, Virginia. I needed that conference because every preacher and every lecturer there was speaking to me and my situation. Our church had been through so much, and I needed some relief. I was so encouraged at that conference. My friend Dr. Donald Porter and I visited First Baptist Church, where Dr. William Booth was the pastor. Dr. Porter knew the pastor, and we were going to see if we could tour their recently completed church building.

The pastor was not in, but the secretary was very gracious and showed us around the building. She also shared with us the process they used to finance the construction. At the time, church bonds were popular in some areas, but I had not heard about financing through church bonds. Not only did the Lord minister to my spirit at the conference, but God also opened another avenue for Friendship to finance the new building.

When I carried the information about church bonds back to our church leaders, they were lukewarm to the idea. But a couple of months later, Deacon Howard Green revisited the concept of church bonds with the Joint Boards. He had learned more about church bonds from First Baptist Church in Huntsville, Alabama. Dr. Julius Scruggs was the pastor and knew the Greens, who were also from Huntsville.

First Baptist had built a beautiful edifice, and they used church bonds to finance their building project. When Deacon Green shared this information with the Joint Boards, the group became excited about the possibility. After all, no bank would even consider loaning us any money to build. The opposition made sure that no bank in the Atlanta area would consider working with Friendship at all.

On January 21, 1994, the opposition filed another motion, and on January 23, the court issued a final order to vote on my tenure, which would take place on January 27, just four days after the court order. God once again came to my rescue. It was the third time the church had voted whether to retain or relieve me of my service. But after the church voted to retain my services, the trouble still was not over because the plaintiffs failed to dismiss their action. This inaction, after having to agree to abide by the majority vote, only demonstrated the lack of integrity and character of this group.

Finally, it appeared that there were cracks forming in the wall of resistance. On February 14, 1994, Attorney William D. Strickland withdrew as counsel for the plaintiff/appellants. A few within the group also withdrew as plaintiffs: Ardell Walcott, Laura Young, Annie M. Miller, Willie Smith, and Wilfred Leaks. It appeared that some were getting tired of fighting but not winning. Others, however, were willing to fight on no matter how many court battles they lost. I just don't know any other way to say this, but God's hand was all over me! I was protected! Strickland was their fifth attorney.

We did not just sit idly and twiddle our thumbs during this period. Attorney Bobby D. Simmons, a member and attorney for the defendants, Donald Earl Bryant and James R. Price, filed a motion for sanctions against the plaintiffs: Will Leroy Grimes, Teddy L. Price (the brother of

James R. Price), Kirby Ragins, Wilfred Leaks, Milton Tucker, Charlie S. W. Rainey, Minnie P. Rainey, Willie Jones, Harry Gibbs, Willie Smith, Charles Glenn, and Susan Ball.

On April 6, 1994, Antonio L. Thomas (the sixth attorney) filed his appearance as counsel for the plaintiff/appellants. After several appeal extensions, the case landed on the Court of Appeals docket on November 21, 1995.

Meanwhile, on July 19, 1994, the same plaintiffs filed another motion for contempt, for a temporary restraining order and interlocutory injunction. They also included defendants Howard Green (Finance Leader), Louis Bell, and Larry Younginer (Building Committee members), individually and jointly.

Judge Rufe E. McCombs held us in contempt. He ruled the officers should have keys to the building. Judge McCombs ordered the plaintiffs' names back on the church bulletin and required us to announce it in church. However, Attorney Simmons argued that Judge McCombs' court did not have jurisdiction over the matter. Attorney Simons included Friendship as a defendant and Donald Earl Bryant and James R. Price and filed an appeal to Judge McCombs' order on September 14, 1994.

On October 13, 1994, Judge Alice D. Bonner granted the defendants' request for summary judgment. She ruled the plaintiffs did not follow statutory procedures for claims against churches under Georgia Nonprofit Corporation Code. The plaintiffs did not raise any factual issues regarding their allegations of fraud. She noted the case had been pending for about a year and addressed in various motions and petitions for restraining orders by six judges.

It seemed as if we were making some progress and were able to get other church people involved. On January 24, 1995, Dr. Joseph Roberts of Ebenezer Baptist Church of Atlanta was appointed as our mediator. The judge and the mediator agreed that the election process would serve as a final resolution to all disputes between the parties. On January 27, 1995, Judge Hull entered and filed the last order of ratification and final judgment on the election and church officers' issues.

It was amazing to me to see how the legal tactics had kept the church in court. There was a need to define "majority" and "membership." I must admit that I was growing weary during this process, but God continued to strengthen me. I talked with members while the legal battle raged. I sought to encourage them. I could only imagine what they were going through. I mentioned earlier that when we defeated one group, another would emerge. Some people who once opposed each other had joined forces and were now on the same side against me.

On February 20, 2001, the tables turned. Deacon James Price and Deacon Larry Younginer joined Eddie Clark, J.D. Hightower, Glover Bolton, Johnny Thompson, Willie R. Philpot, Rufus Jordan, and L. M. Smith. They filed a motion for a temporary restraining order against Donald Earl Bryant and Deacon William Howard Green, Sr., who was now chairman of deacons. That same day, the plaintiffs filed for a motion for special appointment of process server. Daldred A. Mason was appointed process server, and a restraining order was issued against Donald Earl Bryant.

Gail S. Tusan set a hearing for the next day, February 21, at 1:00 p.m. I had noticed but had been unable to understand—and I am not trying to abrogate myself in all of this—but it appeared that all our conflicts had something to do with the building process. The first building involved John Cox and others when we wanted to purchase the sixty-six acres of land. It was John Cox, Ted Price, and the Trustees.

When we moved toward building the educational building, it was Louis Bell, Jesse Pugh, Howard Seals, and others. I decided not to have a third phase building committee. However, God was showing us how to build through conflict and keep ministries moving. God was also proving that we could build debt-free!

On February 23, 2001, Judge Gail S. Tusan denied the plaintiff's motion for a restraining order against Donald Earl Bryant and recommended mediation. March 28, 2001, there was another vote on my tenure ordered by the court. Officers from New Era State Baptist Convention and Fulton County Court appointees were present to validate the votes. This election was the fourth vote on my tenure; the tally was 528 who voted to retain me as pastor and 350 who voted no. My margin of victory was dwindling, some of the people had left the church and others were tired.

Much of our energy went to navigate our ministry through this nonsense. This fight was a major attack against the faith community. One of the most critical and disheartening things to happen with this conflict was that other churches could see if they disagreed with the pastor, all they had to do was go to court. But with God's blessing, while we were fighting off their attacks, the Lord was still working.

I am reminded of the Israelites at the Red Sea when Pharaoh and his army pursued Israel after God delivered them from Egypt's oppressive land. When Israel realized that they were blocked in by the Red Sea in front of them and mountains on the left and right, they had no way out with Pharaoh's army chasing from behind. The Bible explains while the Israelites were afraid and panicking, Moses said to them, "Stand still, and see the salvation of the LORD" (Exodus 14:13). But we are also told that while all of this was going on, God was working!

Although it appeared that we were being tossed to and fro', and we were, God was still at work in our deliverance. What is so amazing to me is that I never lost the gift of faith. I always believed that God would bring to reality the vision and dreams given to me. I am so impressed with what God can do with a fragile human being in times of trouble.

One of the greatest gifts God gave us was the employment of Deaconess Janice Scott as church secretary. Her tenure started midway through the conflict. She had been a member of Friendship since the middle 1980s and was able to see all that had transpired. She was the daughter of a pastor and knew something about conflict and hierarchy in the church. Friendship employed her because she was not a part of the minority. She trusted the vision yet also was able to stay out of the politics in the church. She had a gift that gave her acceptance with everyone on both sides.

I had established an intern ministry for seminary students, and we had three at the time. Minister Deborah Broughton was a student at Candler School of Theology and an excellent preacher and administrator. She assisted Janice in the church office. As an intern, she proved to be just what we needed.

Shortly after I became pastor, Deacon Green told me that God would send me everything and everyone I needed to move the ministry forward. And from my first day as pastor until my last, God did exactly that! Minister Broughton was an energetic, informative, and exciting preacher, and her administrative skills were equally impressive.

The office staff was obligated and directed to serve everyone regardless of their politics. People from both sides were requesting copies, postings, and other services. However, I had to approve their work, and I would never endorse anything that I thought was political or damaging to the church. I had to send out letters to our church members to update them on our church's happenings. Sometimes the opposition was putting out false information, and I found myself scrambling to put out those fires. There were times when we did not have a lot of time to respond, but the office staff proved able to meet every challenge.

May 11, 2001: Deacon James Price, Plaintiffs, et al., filed a Complaint about Equitable Relief. May 21, 2001, Judge John J. Goger ordered that defendants William Howard Green and Donald Earl Bryant appear before the court on May 25, 2001, at 9:30 a.m. to consider a temporary restraining order and the appointment of a receiver.

June 8, 2001: William Howard Green and Donald Earl Bryant filed answer and counterclaim. On June 12, 2001, Judge John J. Goger granted in part and denied the request for a preliminary injunction. The court denied the plaintiff's request for a receiver. Mediation is to be scheduled.

June 28, 2001: Plaintiffs and defendants met for mediation, but Deacon William Howard Green and Pastor Donald Earl Bryant received information that only those named as plaintiffs and defendants would be present with the mediator. The plaintiffs brought their attorney, and several church members not listed in the court documents; therefore, we decided not to participate.

July 2, 2001: Plaintiffs motion to hold defendants Bryant and Green in contempt. The plaintiffs' request for a preliminary injunction be granted in part and denied in part. Signed, Judge John J. Goger.

July 8, 2001: Defendants Green and Bryant submitted a Request for Oral Hearing.

July 13, 2001: Defendant Bryant filed a Motion for Protective Order.

March 18, 2003: Defendants Green and Bryant's motion to dismiss came before Judge Stephanie B. Manis. She dismissed this complaint in its entirety.

The opposition got the court to agree to another election of the pastor; the vote in favor of retaining me was overwhelming. The church leaders managed this re-reelection. The Lord blessed Deacon Howard Green to be in place as chairman of the deacons; and the Lord used him to save me. The majority and most vocal deacons wanted me gone, other relatively new deacons had not been in place a year and were not very vocal.

One of the deacons said in the meeting, "I move for the pastor's tenure." As chairman, Deacon Green stood and said, "I am not going to carry that motion. What has he done?" As chair, he refused to entertain that motion. If he had not been in that position, Donald Earl Bryant would have been history. But God is faithful! God can do what no other power can do. God can use whomever God pleases, and in this situation, God used Deacon Green.

On March 18, 2003, Judge Stephanie B. Manis dismissed the plaintiff's action against the deacon's chairman, William Howard Green, and Pastor Donald Earl Bryant in its entirety. After years of being hog-tied by the opposition's legal strategy, Pastor Bryant, Deacon Green, and the Friendship Baptist Church were free at last! Or so we thought!

The plaintiffs could not prove the charges brought against us. The court upheld the expulsion of seven deacons in April 2003. And not a single check was presented with Pastor Bryant's signature, so they could not prove their fraud claim.

Deacon Green had advised me in 1991 that I did not need a key to the church finance room, nor did I ever need to sign a check. That counsel proved to be invaluable over time, mainly because we had a very competent and trusted finance ministry in place. Secondly, the plaintiffs were not able to produce one check with my signature.

With all the court activities and distractions around the church, the Lord was able to hold it together. One of our mothers, Mary Redding, said of me (with others standing in hearing distance), "The Lord got glue in his shoes. He can't go anywhere." Mother Redding used that analogy to justify how I was able to stand through it all. Still, I think that a sermon preached about Joshua and Israel's faithfulness best describes our situation. Not only was I standing, but others as well, including Mother Redding, holding on to our faith!

✝✝✝

SERMON
"Faith Makes the Difference"

Joshua 6:1–7,20 (NIV): Now the gates of Jericho were securely barred because of the Israelites. No one went out and no one came in. ²Then the LORD said to Joshua, "See, I have delivered Jericho into your hands, along with its king and fighting men. ³March around the city once with all the armed men. Do this for six days. ⁴Have seven priests carry trumpets of rams' horns in front of the Ark. On the seventh day, march around the city seven times, with the priests blowing the trumpets. ⁵When you hear them sound a long blast on the trumpets, have the whole army give a loud shout; then the wall of the city will collapse and the army will go up, everyone straight in." ⁶So Joshua son of Nun called the priests and said to them, "Take up the ark of the covenant of the LORD and have seven priests carry trumpets in front of it." ⁷And he ordered the army, "Advance! March around the city, with an armed guard going ahead of the ark of the LORD."

²⁰When the trumpets sounded, the army shouted, and at the sound of the trumpet, when the men gave a loud shout, the wall collapsed; so everyone charged straight in, and they took the city.

This text is ideal for people who are facing an impossible situation. It is incredible to see how people in so many instances will turn to everything and everyone except the One who can intervene and change their situation. And what I have learned is that if God does not change the situation; God will give you a different attitude about that situation.

What you thought at one time was working against you is now seen as a blessing for you. The God we serve can do the impossible! If you don't give up on God, God will never give up on you. And you know, I love this about God, God is full of mercy and grace. God does not have anger hangovers. Wherever you are in life, God will meet you there. You cannot be too low, nor can you be too high for God's infinite mercy and grace to reach you. There are no substitutes for God. Only God can do what God does. Don't be fooled by smooth talk and empty promises. Only God can be God.

Why do you think people get addicted to different things? They are trying to resolve unresolved issues in their lives. Something is missing, and they are trying to fill that void with drugs, relationships, material things, and psychological deceptions. But when you need a miracle in your life, when you need a supernatural move, you need God; and it is faith in God that makes the difference!

In this text, Joshua has now taken over leadership of the Israelites. Moses, his faithful and dedicated predecessor, has done what we all must do at some point—he has run his race and has finished his course. Joshua is now leading the people to the Promised Land, the land flowing with milk and honey. There is one thing that we learn from Joshua, and we should never forget it, and that is if God has ever done anything for you, if God has ever worked a miracle in your life, you must unequivocally believe that God can do it again. God may not do it, but the blessing is in knowing that God can.

God had already proven that the impossible is possible. Joshua was there at the Red Sea when the Egyptian army pursued them, and they found themselves between two mountains (or a rock and a hard place). The Egyptians were behind them and the Red Sea in front of them. He saw God part the sea, allowing them to cross over on dry land. Remember, it was Joshua who first went and spied out the land of Canaan. Joshua and Caleb were the two who brought back a favorable report. Twelve went out, but ten did not see how they could have the victory. When the ten saw the people of the land, they saw themselves as grasshoppers. They saw a fortified city that made penetration impossible.

But Joshua, without a doubt, knew that whatever God promised would come to pass. Maybe he did not know how, but he surely knew that God would. Although the odds to the natural eye seemed stacked against them, Joshua knew that all things are possible with God. And now Israel is faced with invading Jericho, a walled city. The city was difficult to invade, and the method God commanded Joshua employ to lead the charge sounded even more impossible.

Let me tell you, if God tells you to do something—I don't mean that if you had too many drinks, or you ate too late one night and had a weird dream—but if God tells you something, regardless of how it sounds, have faith in God. God tells Joshua to command the people to march around Jericho's walls once a day for six days. On the seventh day, they were to march around the wall seven times. On that seventh time, God instructed them to shout and the walls would come down. Wow! Can you imagine being told to march around a city for seven days, and after that, shout, and the walls will come tumbling down? No bombs, no cannons, sticks, or stones—just shout! But the people had faith in God. It was faith that made the difference, so they did as God commanded and the walls came down.

The wall came down because the people had faith in God. Faith made the difference! The situation seemed impossible, but with faith in God your impossible situations will fall. Recently, we were in biblical application study in the "How to Follow Jesus" class and we began to talk about faith. I asked, "Do you believe that you can raise the dead?"

A couple of outspoken people said they did not believe they could raise dead people. We read John 14:12 and the following passages. I also told them about the faith and work I have done in hospitals. I told them when I go to hospitals, I expect two things: healing for the people and dead people to be raised! That is my expectation. We have many members in Friendship, and we do not average four funerals a year. That is not by happenstance; that is because I pray that they do not die. Now if you don't believe me, and some of you don't, give me your name and I will see if God and I can prove a point.

The reality is Jesus did not raise every person who died, but we do see that Jesus was able to do what others could not. I said to one of the class members, "I sure hope I do not die around you because you do not have the faith that God can use you to raise me."

When one embraces faith in God, you start with the premise that regardless of what it is, it is possible with God! In John 14:12, Jesus said, "Truly, truly I say to you, he who believes in Me will do the works that I do also. And he will do greater works than these, because I am going to My Father."

I don't know what your situation might be, but I know that if you have faith in God, God can turn your situation around. Faith makes the difference! There is nothing too hard for God. God can do the impossible.

It might seem as if you are facing irreversible odds, but God can turn your situation around. Ask the woman with the issue of blood (Mark 5:25–34). She said within herself, "If I just touch his clothes, I will be made well."

Also, in that class a woman gave a testimony that she had begun to develop symptoms, and her sister said, "This looks like lupus." Because of how she was feeling and skin irritations, she went to the doctor, who made the same assessment. She took several exams, and the findings showed signs of lupus. After leaving the doctor, she talked with God and said, "God, I have been getting ready for retirement, and I do not want to deal with this issue in my retirement."

She went back to the doctor, and they tested her again. When the results came back, there was no sign of what they had seen on her previous visit. Please, please don't tell me what God cannot do! God can work a miracle in your life.

So, Joshua led the Israelites around Jericho's wall, and on the seventh day and the seventh time, they shouted, and the walls came down! The walls did not come down because of base and baritone voices. Faith in God brought those walls down. Faith makes the difference. God commanded, and they did what God said. They could not understand it either, but they were walking by faith.

One day, two blind men followed Jesus, crying unto him "Lord, Son of David, have mercy on us!" Jesus went into the house, and the blind men came to him. Jesus asked them, "What do you want me to do for you?"

They said, "We want our sight." Jesus had compassion on them and touched their eyes. They received their sight and followed him (Matthew 20:29–34).

Faith makes the difference! If you have faith in God, God will do the impossible in your life. Jesus had faith in God. That is why He went to the cross at Calvary because of his faith in God. He believed God would use him to die for the sins of the world and on the third day, raise Him to life again.

Faith makes the difference. Faith works! And as you know, when you call upon the name of God in faith, God will be there. The Lord is there because it is faith that moves the hand of God! It is faith in God that makes the difference! Amen!

✝✝✝

In 1989, Brenda and I purchased a home on Enon Road. In 1994, I met Cary Wynn, a contractor who was building a mansion for a family right down the street. After talking with Mr. Wynn, I learned that he had constructed a house that I admired in Southwest Atlanta. He told me that he could go over the plans with Brenda and me, and we could see where we would go from there. He came by our home one Sunday evening to show us the projects and told me that house would cost over a half-million dollars (which was well out of our price range). He knew another builder who was building a smaller version of the same house. The next week I drove over to see the house, and it looked nothing like the house I had admired from the outside. But when I walked into that house, I thought it was one of the most beautiful homes I had ever seen. I had to show it to Brenda. The next day, the builder allowed us to walk through as they were doing touch-up painting.

Brenda was also extremely impressed with the house. As we were leaving, we stood at the front entrance and I told her, "I can build this house." That got the wheels turning in my mind. I had never built a house before, but after working with my brothers, Bug and Buddy, and believing what my father told me over the years, I thought I could do it. I see now how working around our family home and with my brothers contributed significantly to my ability to spearhead building the campus at Friendship and our home.

I went back to that house several times, and Melvin Cooper allowed me to take pictures. The home was so beautiful and incredibly detailed. I took pictures of everything because that house was just that impressive to me. I have always believed that there was never a reason to reinvent something, but rather customize it to your liking. So, I purchased the architect's plans to build our house, cut and pasted rooms and the garage, had the plans copied as I liked, and then moved forward with planning to develop our new home.

So, we started looking for property to build our home. Carolyn Woods, a member of our church, was our real estate agent looking for a property. She took us to East Point, and at the end of the street were five acres with only eight other houses on the street. The property looked as though it had been abandoned for years. The Century 21® sale sign had rotted and fallen.

We were able to purchase that property at an excellent price. The price was so low that it caused me to investigate whether this property was a previous waste site! Upon investigation, I found out that the property was fine, and we still live in that house today and enjoy our home.

We continued to move forward with our church building plans despite the ongoing opposition and the litigation. God was on our side and gave us breakthrough at every turn.

We submitted plans to the architect to build our church, based on an idea gleaned from the House of Hope, where Dr. E. Dewey Smith is pastor. Deacon Willie Chavers and I went to Chapel Hill Church one evening, and he took pictures of that building. While I knew that we could not build a church of that magnitude, I did get some ideas regarding what we wanted our facility to resemble. When I sat down with the architect and shared with him our thoughts, we arrived at the rendering we now have for our church.

Like Solomon, I was not only leading construction at the Lord's house, I was also building our own home at the same time. Brenda helped because for almost a year while we were building our house, she only came to the property twice. Because she trusted me to proceed with building our home, we were able to make swift progress. Having seen the house we were building in real-time, she said, "I like peach and green." Our roof and carpet are green, and our master bedroom is peach.

I went to Gilford Forest and saw a beige stucco house with a green shingled roof, so I decided that was the color combination for us. After I took Brenda by to see it, she approved, and we were on our way. She gave me the freedom to build and not haggle over every detail of the house we were building. I don't know how I did it, but I found myself spending a lot of time at the church, a lot of time at our new home site, and a lot of time in ministry. The reality is (without claiming to be overly spiritual) God did it!

As God was blessing us at the church and with our own home, God saw fit to bless our lives with something that was both exciting and surprising. We learned in October 1995 that Brenda was pregnant. Our family and the church were surprised as well. It was a welcomed announcement

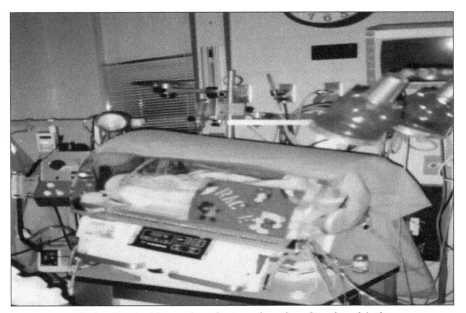

Baby Rachel in an incubator shortly after her birth

and addition to our family. People at the church had begun to refer to us as Abraham and Sarah because I was 45 years old and Brenda was 40 when she gave birth to Rachel.

On January 16, 1996, I had a meeting at the church with a Audria Dunson, a young adult member. During our meeting, I got a call from my wife. "I think my water has broken." The baby was not due for another four months. Our baby Rachel was born that night weighing one pound and seven ounces. After Brenda obtained her release from the hospital, she went to the hospital every day for four months to visit and nurse our daughter.

Simultaneously, the sanctuary was under construction, and I had to make several changes with workers and management. One day I was walking around the building and noticed that the crew laying the bricks was not laying them straight. We were paying the foreman Paul and Associates had hired to supervise the job $2,500 per week!

Captain Louis Bell, a trustee and a Delta airlines pilot, served as the building committee chairman. He lived about a mile from the church and was able to visit the site almost daily. He would come by the area dressed in his captain's uniform whenever he was leaving the airport. Everyone knew he was a pilot. When he was not in uniform, he would come dressed in his Texas hat and cowboy boots. I think he was deeply committed to the work but not focused on the expenditure of money, and we were getting low on cash, with only about fifty percent of the project done. The cash flow issue caught my attention was when I learned from Deacon Howard Green how much money remained for the project, and I knew how much money was needed to complete the project.

We were spending money on light poles, yet the exterior and interior of the building remained unfinished. We needed to direct our resources more responsibly.

We had a meeting with Paul and Associates and terminated their management agreement and the supervisor, but we kept the architect. Now it was up to Friendship to manage the building of our sanctuary, and I took full responsibility for completing the project because the Lord was with me.

Deacon Green and I met with Louis and informed him that we would restructure the financial oversight. The three of us, (Captain Bell, Deacon Green, and I) would have to approve any spending. We were at a point where we could not pay the grader, the electrician, the plumbers, and pavers as scheduled. We were using revenues from Sunday's tithes and offerings to pay contractors and staff members as well. Deacon Green and I decided to meet with contractors and work out payment arrangements. I told Deacon Green privately, "We can't run out of money."

I thought if we could give the contractors a percentage of their pay, they would continue to work. They all agreed to accept what we were able to pay, and the work continued. Then there came a Sunday when we could not fully compensate the staff. The church was not informed of our immediate financial situation. Such information would only lend fuel to our opposition. We managed the situation.

I decided to forgo my salary for that month, and everyone else got paid. Then, we decided to move payday from Sundays to Wednesdays to have receipts from tithes and offerings available by Wednesday.

I also learned an incredibly important lesson about construction processes that would help us with future building projects. I noticed that all the contractors received payment on Friday, whether they completed the work or not. We employed a different strategy when undertaking subsequent facilities. I will say more about this process later.

What I am about to share is hard for many readers to believe, but Deacon Green and I know it to be true. One month when we were running short of funds, Deacon Green and I met at the church one Friday night; as always, we prayed. We prayed that God would open another door to cover the debts we obligated ourselves to pay. We are both men of faith, and we had confidence in God. What God did was add another Sunday to that month so that we could meet our obligations. I know many would say, "How could that be true?" It's not something that can be explained in earthly terms. All I know is that God did it!

Our calendar might show one thing, but our calendars do not bind God. By having that extra Sunday, we could pay our debt and not damage our credibility. God did it! The work continued, and we could see the people's optimism and excitement build as cars drove by every day. The people were preparing to claim their new sanctuary. I saw some of the naysayers slowly moving over to support the effort. The reality was that we were all in this together, and I realized that we could not have done what we were doing if just one of the persons involved was not in our midst.

One evening when I left the church after trying to oversee the work, I was alone in my car driving up the hill. "I am tired of this!" I said. The Lord responded and simply said, "You don't have to do it!"

I immediately said, "Forgive me, Lord!" I realized that God did not have to use me; but rather, I was blessed to be a part of this move of God. God was doing something unique, and God decided to use me. Although it seemed like moving to our new church home was just obstacle after obstacle, I had experienced God bringing us through every one of them. Now was not time to give up.

October 19, 1997, the Friendship Baptist Church moved into a new sanctuary located at 4141 Old Fairburn Road. The pain was worth the gain! It was an exciting day for the church. After everything we had been through, this day was worth all we endured.

The motorcade started at the old site, moving down Camp Creek Parkway to the new location. By the time some of us had reached the new edifice, the last car was leaving the old site parking lot, which was a distance of approximately five miles.

Through it all, God is faithful!

The photograph is evidence of the level of participation in opening day. I decided not to preach that day for several reasons, and one was that those who were opposed to me could not use me as their excuse not to come and worship. I had gotten to know Dr. C. Mackey Daniels as he was the sitting president of the Progressive National Baptist Convention. He knew all about Friendship and our struggles, and he was happy to come and preach for us.

Because of our struggles, there were several prominent personalities who came to share in our celebration: Ambassador Andrew Young, Dr. Joseph Lowery, Representative John Lewis, Dr. Howard Creecy, Sr., Dr. Gardner Taylor, Jennifer Holiday, Dr. Joseph L. Roberts, Pastor Harold Baker of the New Era Convention, Pastor Willie Bodrick, Pastor Tyrell Brown, Dr. Tyrone Pitts, and many others. We had two weeks of powerful worship and celebration of the things God had done.

Although we were in a worshipful celebration, we continued to be involved with court battles. The court activity moved us to address everything the

**Pastor Bryant welcoming members on the opening day
of the new church edifice.**

courts exposed in our constitution and bylaws, so we amended it to fill the cracks that had allowed the courts to have free rein in our church. We also found it necessary to put in writing the kind of behavior that would lead to a member's expulsion. First and foremost, if a member brings an action before the court against the church or another member without the church's authority and support, expulsion will immediately take place the minute the court document is signed. When that person leaves the courthouse, they are no longer a member of Friendship.

On January 16, 2001, the church voted to amend the bylaws, replacing the joint boards with a church council. I also learned something about my management style. While I would like to think of myself as a hands-off leader, I wanted to know everything involving the church. Deacon Green, chairman of the deacons' ministry, said to a church member, "I don't want anyone to tell me anything about the church that they do not want the pastor to know." In other words, if he knew something involving the church, he felt that it was his duty to inform the pastor. That statement opened my understanding of how important it was to know everything possible about the movement and decisions made that impacted the church. I felt that no ministry was an island; not one of them stood alone.

Pastor Bryant with two Friendship youth

Chapter Six
How to Build a Church Debt Free

Friendship Community Church

As you have read in my sermon "Vision," God placed in my spirit that we would be able to construct a new campus financed by God's people; in other words, debt-free. I had no clue about how that would occur, but I believed that God knew. As you read through this chapter, there is absolutely no way that I would have known how we could build debt-free.

We tried to get a bank loan, and it appeared that everything was working in our favor. We had all the information needed for the loan application. The committee reached out to several banks. At least two banks told us that they had received letters from church members stating that they did not want to secure a loan and that the church was in dispute. Those banks were not interested in getting involved in lending to a congregation in quarrel.

Finally, we went to Citizens Trust in Atlanta, where some of the church's members were employees and board members. Citizens Trust is an African-American owned bank, and we felt good about being approved for a $3.5 million loan to build the sanctuary, which would seat 3,500 people. We went through the loan process, which included $5,000 in earnest money, but the bank reneged on the day set for closing.

I believe that it was a set up to kill our spirit and cause renewed conflict in the church, and we never got the earnest money back. We should have known that this could have happened because there were persons with the opposition who had remarkably close ties with the bank.

What a blow!

While we were inside the bank on the scheduled closing day, we learned that the bank had denied the loan. But what I have learned about God is that at every turn, God is faithful. If one door is closed, God will move to another. And if that door closes, God will open a window. And if the window closes, God will construct a new building. God is awesome! God is faithful!

God encouraged all the members of the building committee not to lose heart, but rather to continue praying and looking for other possibilities. I stated earlier how after visiting Dr. William Booth's church I learned of the usage of church bonds. After some additional research on church bonds, God led us to Church Mutual, a company based in Texas.

We contacted them, and their representatives came and made a presentation to us on how to secure the $3.5 million needed to complete phase one. Their representative Rosalyn, an African-American woman, led the presentation. Rosalyn was very thorough and extremely professional in her presentation. She was brilliant and deeply knowledgeable about the product she was presenting to us. As a part of her presentation, we learned that selected members of the building committee would have to learn how to present the program to other church members and enroll them.

Once the team was ready, Church Mutual prepared written material and explained the church's investment options. Church Mutual designed brochures for Friendship, with options ranging from six months to fifteen years. The interest rates were 6 percent simple interest to 10.5 percent compounded daily. There were four days per week set aside to reach our goal of $3.5 million. Members of the committee were present to assist interested persons on Mondays, Tuesdays, Thursdays, and Fridays. Anyone who wanted to participate in the bond program could do so, and non-members were not excluded from participation. Upon presentation of the Bond offering, people stood in line to sign up.

The momentum was on our side to build and the people started to invest in church bonds. Some withdrew monies from their retirement accounts at work because they wanted to support the church, and the return of simple and compound interest was attractive. People were investing in their children and grandchildren. Within six weeks we had reached our goal, and now we could move to the next step of the process.

Once we sold the bonds, we used Reliance Trust Company to manage the Friendship Church bonds. One of the areas I never really got involved in was finance. I did not think I needed to know the details regarding the finance ministry. I had more than enough confidence in the people who worked in that ministry. Deacon Howard Green put a structure in place within the church where accountability, checks, and balances were paramount. Deacon Green was deputy budget director at the Centers for Disease Control (CDC). He knew the work and he genuinely loved the Lord.

The primary reason I believe that God allowed us to build debt-free is that we were faithful. The people who led our ministry and those who served in the finance ministry were good stewards of what God gave us. I had learned from my father not to be wasteful. Whenever an opportunity presented itself, he would say, "Now is the time to put the whip to the horse." But more critically, Jesus has promised, *"you have been faithful over a few things, I will make you ruler over many things"* (Matthew 25:23).

The people of Friendship were faithful. We were able to purchase sixty-six acres that were ideally located, but the initial frontage needed was lacking. For the original fifty-two acres we purchased to work for us, we would need to buy the house with fourteen acres that was adjacent to that property. We visited the owner, an older African-American man who lived there with his son. He agreed to sell the house and fourteen acres for $175,000. The sixty-six acres cost the church $375,000, which was paid out of the treasury. The church now had a frontage of fourteen acres at 4141 Old Fairburn Road, College Park, Georgia.

We learned about Paul and Associates, a construction management entity based in Tyler, Texas. This group was constructing three churches in the area—Jackson Memorial on Fairburn Road, New Birth in Decatur, and Big Miller Grove in Lithonia. Thanks to the gracious pastors, our group was able to visit each site. We contracted with Paul and Associates and their architect to design a rendering, which we presented to the congregation. The people were excited about what they saw. Although there were three buildings on the drawing, we knew that we would have to build in phases.

The property was purchased and paid for, the rendering produced, and the construction drawings submitted. The building committee and many in the church were excited about what was happening in their church. There were people on the building committee with some experience from having their homes remodeled, but there were no contractors or builders. In other words, we did not have the kind of in-house knowledge needed to approach a building of this magnitude. We had learned from other churches that their building committees worked hand-in-hand with Paul and Associates. And from the outside looking in, it seemed as though things were going well for them. After securing the funds and having a local company manage the bonds and payouts, we were on our way.

Once the sanctuary construction project started, we thought it would be best to grade all three buildings and complete the parking lot for five hundred and fifty cars. When the foundation crew started on the sanctuary, we also negotiated an excellent price to form and pour the educational building slab.

We learned from building the sanctuary that there were setbacks to using too many trades at one time if you do not have the money to pay for the completed project. We were using the money out of the treasury and managing tithes and offerings to continue a vibrant ministry and build Phase II as the Lord had blessed us with Phase I.

We noticed that no one would get finished with several trades working simultaneously, but it was an expectation that all would get a weekly or bi-weekly payment draws from their base contract. Instead of having all the trades on the job simultaneously (in many instances getting in each other's way), we would have one trade work at a time, except where we required the services of more than one skill. When one trade finished their work to the rough-in point, we could pay them and move to the next contractor.

Throughout the building process, and despite the internal conflict, Friendship dedicated the Charles Jackson Sargent Educational Building on February 23, 2003. Again, there was a group to revolt against the process and the pastor. There were people in the church who were not there to help, but rather, to hinder God's work.

God already had proven what God could do. God's faithfulness also reminds me of Moses leading the Israelites out of the land of Egypt. Although enslaved for 400 years, they could not wait to build an idol god even after Moses had led them out by the power of God. In the same manner, it was amazing to see how some people were not respectful of what God had done for us.

We found ourselves in court again while the educational building was under construction. Some of the people did not honor what God had done. But my faith was too strong to be sidetracked by those seeking visibility or influence over weak-minded people.

God again prevailed! The Charles Jackson Sargent Educational Building was not only constructed but also furnished with banquet tables and chairs and a riser in the fellowship hall, a video projector with remote screen, a chapel seating 250 people with a private screen, classrooms with smart TVs and chairs with desks, an IT (information technology) room, a conference room, a resource center, three furnished offices, a daycare facility, a commercial kitchen, and an elevator.

Charles Jackson Sargent Educational Building

God had blessed us with all of this debt-free! Look at God!

On the Sunday of dedication, I preached the same sermon, "Vision," that was peached in February 1992 when I revealed to the people what God was giving us. I preached that sermon in part to demonstrate that what the Lord had promised, the Lord had done! I deliberately preached the same sermon to prove that what God had shown me years before had now come to fruition.

When the educational facility was complete, we started to construct the Donald Earl Bryant Family Life Center and Sports Complex in 2006. We had graded but not poured the foundation on the site. The Family Life Center consisted of two commercial weight rooms, a children's room, a youth room with a full-sized basketball court, and large male and female restrooms with showers and lockers. There are two professional-sized tennis courts and four other basketball courts on the outside along with a ball field to the west. The process of generating funds for construction was simple. We would use our own money.

Don't forget that the banks had turned their backs on us when we started the sanctuary building project, and I was determined that we would not turn our backs on God. God had brought us through that situation before, so I knew that God could do it again without a doubt. And we built the educational building debt-free.

I never said it, but because of the disciples' persecution in the book of Acts, the Gospel moved beyond Jerusalem and others received the Good News. When the banks would not work with us we used our own money; we used church bonds for the sanctuary with members and friends' funds, and those who invested got great returns. From that, we learned that we could finance our projects and glorify God in the process.

We financed the Charles Jackson Sargent Educational Building through tithes and offerings and faithful stewardship. And now the Donald Earl Bryant Family Life Center and Sports Complex would be funded again by God's people! What would be our strategy?

I did copy the model from Church Mutual. We could not offer bonds, but we did offer what I called The Gift Ministry, which functioned like the bond program. Every member who wanted to give money gave money. At the end of a specified period, we would give back their money with appreciation. Because we set the terms up at different times, we could return all the funds received.

We designated a Sunday when we asked every member to give five hundred dollars. We were trying to generate three hundred thousand dollars to complete the slab and order the third phase's steel. God gave me confidence when I presented this strategy to the church. It was essential to meet our goal for a couple of reasons. We wanted to show that the congregation believed in what we were doing, and we wanted to get started with the project.

Donald Earl Bryant Family Life Center and Sports Complex

The Lord gave me the confidence to present this plan, knowing that a percentage of people would not or could not participate, by reminding me that God had given me all I've ever had. I knew every earthly thing that happened in my life was because of God. For example, I purchased and built our home, it would not have been possible without the church.

The Lord showed me that even if I had to get an equity line of credit or sell my house to generate $300,000, God had provided an avenue for success. God assured me that the following week I could announce to the church that we reached our goal. There was no way we could fail. God had done so many great things through and for me. Walking in faith was all I knew.

4141 Old Fairburn Road
College Park, Georgia 30349-1767
(404) 349-6040
Donald Earl Bryant, Pastor

Gift Ministry Certificate of Receipt

Giver's Name _____

Giver's Address _____

Giver's Telephone _____

Giver's ID _____

Date of Gift _____ Gift's Years _____

Initial Gift $ _____

Return of Gift Date   Return of Gifts $ _____

Beneficiary Name(s) _____

_____

Authorized Signatures

_____   _____

Donald Earl Bryant   Lester Copeland
Pastor   Chairman Deacon Ministry

_____

Alice-Marie Hutchison
Authorized Notary, Church Clerk

Again, understand that our church continued to support outside organizations and in-house ministries. We were not willing to sacrifice ministries that would bless the community for brick and mortar. I believe because of our faithfulness, attitude, and position toward priorities for ministry, God continued to bless the work of our hands. We never cut our community outreach budget throughout these years of conflict.

January 19, 1999, we presented the concept of a church council at the annual church conference. After praying about our structure and decision-making process, the church had moved from deacon controlled to deacon/trustee joint board representatives to rule by deacons, trustees, and Christian education.

Now the Lord was leading me to Acts 15, where Peter addressed the council at Jerusalem, regarding a dilemma he faced in the ministry field and sought guidance from church officials in Jerusalem. This structure gave me the idea of establishing a church council at Friendship.

How would the church council be organized, and who would serve on that council? The one constant that I have found to promote anything that God gave me—it was essential to have biblical support for what I was proposing.

I introduced Acts 15 to the joint boards to show how we could serve as a church council and officially represent the entire church. If a pastor moves according to biblical principles, it would not be with the pastor, but rather with God if there be disagreements. And I have learned that God always wins!

The original thought was to have the leader, assistant leader and secretary from the deacons, trustees, board of Christian education, and three at-large members from the congregation, to equal twelve. We all know that twelve is a significant number in biblical history. There were twelve tribes of Israel; Jesus had twelve disciples; and in the Book of Revelation, there are twelve gates to the holy city. In my thinking, we could limit the council to twelve and the deacons would go for that with the biblical support. This structure would provide full church representation, but most importantly, provide transparency within the church body. Deacon Green and I knew that the deacons would never support a church council's concept if we did not include all members of their board. When we presented it to the joint boards, the deacons made it known that was the key to their support of the new structure.

I presented the church council concept in the church conference to include the positions named above and members, the business manager, finance leader, and all twenty-seven deacons. There was also a requirement for all council members. If a council member missed three unexcused meetings within a year, they would be dismissed from the council with no provision for them to return. All they had to do was to call the office or tell another member of the council or me that they would not be present for the meeting, and some deacons failed to meet that requirement, which led to their dismissal from the council.

The church council met twice a year (March and October) with the other joint meetings continuing their regular schedule. The group decided that the church council meetings should replace the joint meetings, which met once a month.

The conference accepted the new structure and meeting of the church council, and now we were moving to full congregational representation. Any member meeting the criteria for the council would have to submit their request to the church office. Here goes God again!

It seems as if every time we started to have some calm, the Lord showed me something else that I needed to destroy that for sure would cause another stir. Deacon Green and I had a conversation about all the strife and conflict in our church, and he remarked that church fights and splits often happened in Baptist churches.

Deacon Green's father was the chairman of deacons at his Huntsville, Alabama church, and he had this to say about Baptist churches: "There has to be something demonic about the name." He may have been just kidding around, but I took him seriously. Deacon Green had been a part of the Baptist denomination all his life, and for him to say that gave me something to ponder. Although we did not believe that there was something demonic about the name, I thought it had everything to do with Baptist polity.

I was in the Charles Jackson Sargent Educational Building's chapel when the Lord gave me this thought, and I said to God, "Really, Lord, now?"

At the time, we were experiencing a degree of peace, and to even think about changing the name of the church from Baptist would probably create another conflict. Although my faith was strong in the Lord, what about the people? Could they endure another battle?

That conversation with God led to a greater discussion and preparation for a name change for Friendship. I established a group of five to investigate the possibility of a name change, which involved biblical precedence, community acceptance, and observation of other churches that had done a name change.

A couple of churches in the area had done a name change—Salem Bible Church (Pastor Jasper Williams), and Thankful Baptist Church (pastored by Dr. Kerwin Lee who now served at Berean Christian Church, which he founded). Across the country, we saw fewer churches organized as Baptist and others removing the label Baptist. What does the Scripture say about it?

I was looking for something favorable. The word "denomination" itself is a mathematical term that suggests division, separation, or designation. And Jesus prayed in the Gospel of John 17:11, "That they might be one." I would direct your attention to Paul's letter in 1 Corinthians 12:12, and the verses that follow, where he talks about the church like the physical body which has many members but one body.

As a part of my investigation, I thought I would ask people who were members of a Baptist church, "What did it mean to be Baptist?" I started with my mother, and I pushed her to this response, "Donald Earl! I don't know what it means, but whatever it means, I will be one until I die!" My mother died on July 1, 2007, and she died a Baptist.

Interestingly, I interviewed preachers and other church leaders in Baptist churches, and to my surprise a significant number of them were not able to articulate what it meant to be Baptist. After talking with more Baptist pastors, I was ready to present to the church council. When the group came back after investigating the name change, we also led the

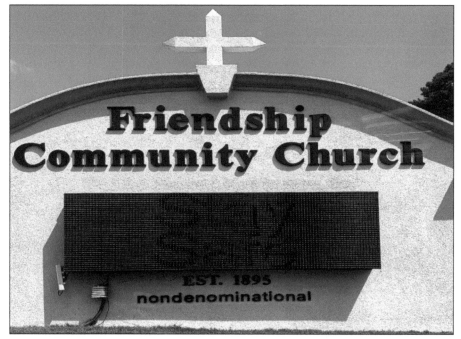

Friendship Community Church Sign

church council in addressing all the titles in the church that were not Bible-based. We stopped calling preachers "Reverend" because there was no biblical evidence that title was ever used in the New Testament Church to identify preachers. I directed the council to look at Psalm 111:9 (KJV) "He sent redemption unto his people: he hath commanded his covenant forever: holy and reverend is his name."

The only place we saw the word "reverend" referred to God and it was in the King James Version of the Bible. We decided not to use that title for preachers because it was not biblical. We also did title changes for "boards" and "committees" instead; we used the title "ministries." These changes were reflected in our revised constitution and bylaws.

The majority of the church council was interested in the discussion, and it went better than I thought. I presented the Greek word, koinonia, which means "fellowship and community," and we agreed on Friendship Community Church. Neighborhoods sprang up all around our site, and that gave additional support to community; now the church became nondenominational.

When I presented it to the church conference, the name change was overwhelmingly accepted. There were only a couple who expressed concern or spoke out against the name change. One thought that we had been Baptist too long to change; the other said that he had been Baptist all his life.

Two families left the church because of the name change, but neither spoke out in the meeting. Conversely, others kept coming and uniting with the church. Some of the new members told me that they came to Friendship because they saw "nondenominational" on our marquee.

God continued to test and prepare me. Two deaths hit me hard in the middle of this ministry process. First, I lost my sister Sandra, whom we called "San," and Dolomite's darling. Everyone loved her because she was thoughtful and caring. She was the type who would come home from college and go visit all the older people in our community.

I remember one visit to my mother's house when San was also there. I had been experiencing some financial difficulties but was trying to handle the situation on my own. We were sitting and talking as I was beating around the bush, trying to talk up some support without asking directly. The more I spoke, San picked up on something that was not right, but my mother did not. San said plainly, "Momma, he doesn't have anywhere to live."

San knew I was homeless. Momma asked what I needed, and then called John Sanders, a family friend who always had money. She asked him to

Donald and Brenda Bryant with Sandra and Clarence Jones

Deacon Howard Green, Sr.

loan her five hundred dollars so that I could go back to Atlanta and have a roof over my head.

San suffered from colon cancer for six years while maintaining an active lifestyle. Sandra Jean Bryant Jones died on August 3, 2006.

Two months later, on the evening of October 23, 2006, I got a telephone call. I just knew it was something about Howard Green. I did not answer the phone. I had no reason to think that he had died because he had not been ill. But that is what I felt.

He and his wife were on vacation at their timeshare in Orlando, but I did not answer the phone because I was anxious about what I would hear. Deacon Green and his wife, Ms. Sugar, had allowed my family to stay at their timeshare for a week, and we had so much fun! Brenda and I took our daughter Rachel, two grandchildren, Isaiah, Rebekah, and a friend, Tenae. It was the best week I had ever spent with Rachel and the grandchildren.

The telephone rang again, so I answered it. Arthur Green, Deacon Howard Green's brother from Montgomery, Alabama, told me that Howard had died. I could not believe it, yet somehow I already knew that he was dead before receiving the official word. It is my understanding that he went to sleep while watching a football game and later woke up and told his wife, "That was the best sleep I had ever had." He went back into the other room to finish watching the game. He fell asleep again and never woke up. I heard people say, "When I die, I want to die like Deacon Green." What I have noticed is that there is no one in line to die like Deacon Green. Just as Deacon Howard Green said to me some years before, "God will give you everything you will need."

Deacon Henry Carter was in place and accepted the deacon's lead position the next day. And just like Howard, Deacon Henry Carter proved to be a faithful soldier. These two brothers were tremendously

The Theatre

gifted and were more than willing to use their gifts and resources to the glory of God without hesitation.

Friendship will never know the value of these two men working with the pastor and the church to help navigate a powerful ministry. I can honestly say we would not have been able to do the things we have done without them, but I am delighted that we did not have to try.

Praise the Lord! After San's death and then Deacon Green's, I said to God, "Why would you do this to me? Two of the most influential people in my life you have taken!"

These are precisely the words God said to me: "Don't think of yourself so highly. Do you believe what happened was because of you?"

Then I said, "Forgive me, Lord! Thank you."

One Sunday, I left the sanctuary service before preaching and walked over to the New Generation Children and Youth Church in the family life center. The leaders were attempting to show a video to the children, but the sun shone through the windows, obscuring their view.

The next Sunday, I went over again and they had a trustee to place black plastic over the twenty-foot tall windows. The Lord spoke to me, "How can you allow such a beautiful building to lose its solemnity by hanging plastic over windows?" That is when the Lord revealed to me a Children and Youth Worship and Recreation Center. We had about fifty-five untouched acres, and we needed another building for our children and youth. I got the name for the building from the children, "The Theatre."

I was preparing for retirement, but I thought we could build The Theatre before I did. When I shared this vision with the children and youth ministry leaders, they were excited about the possibilities. I later presented it to the church council, and they, too, were excited about the vision. I had spoken with Pastor Dailey previously, and he also was willing to support the effort. I explained to him how we would approach this venture in terms of our responsibilities. For the most part, he had managed the church's work, including worship services, Bible studies, and everything else going on at Friendship. I asked him to take care of the church, and I would spend my time constructing The Theatre. I felt extremely comfortable with this arrangement because it would only lend itself to having a smooth pastoral transition.

Over the years, the church had learned to trust me, despite many years of litigation. They knew that I would always do what was in the church's best interest and that I would be a good steward. Once I learned what the construction costs would be from a couple of quality bids, I told the council and the church that we could save $1.5 million. We had two things going for us—we had some money to get started, and we had time.

Throughout the building process, another vital aspect of the project was that we sought some of our people to participate. Church members must eat just like others. It is so ridiculous to see so many of our churches building and spending millions of dollars with so little of it going back into the African-American community. There are too few of our people in the building trade because we don't allow them to develop their skills. In every building project at Friendship, there has been significant African-American participation.

I was getting closer to retirement and had to think about my financial needs after retirement. I did not want to put my family's welfare in someone else's hands. I know how excited young preachers can be, especially with a large ministry like Friendship. I did not want to bring a successor on board whose "vision" could include abolishing established support vehicles that would negatively impact my retirement or that of other staff persons on Friendship's retirement plan.

It was vital for me to put into place the support I would need to maintain our family's lifestyle. Thanks to Deacons Green and Carter for providing the leadership in establishing a retirement plan for me. Although the program would not provide the needed level of income, Deacon Carter led the church council in establishing a retirement plan for employees of the church, which would supplement other provisions like IRAs and Social Security. We gave all vested employees a percentage of their base pay as a retirement benefit.

Pastor Dailey was a tremendous help when it came to me becoming pastor emeritus of the church. When I presented the church council with a proposal to become pastor emeritus upon my retirement, I confess that I did not know the functions of a pastor emeritus. In the middle of my stumbling to explain, Pastor Dailey jumped in and clarified the council's understanding.

The church council agreed to the position of pastor emeritus and made plans to present it to the church conference. The church conference accepted the church council's recommendation, and now I am pastor emeritus at the Friendship Community Church.

In the transition process, I observed Pastor Dailey's interactions, preaching, and teaching. I had experienced him implementing ministries that enhanced the church's outreach, in-house ministries, and vision for the future. Pastor Dailey wanted to implement serving lunch during our midday Bible study and dinner during our evening Bible study which he rebranded, "Revive Wednesdays."

I was lukewarm to the idea because I thought that we ate too much at the church already. But it was his vision, and I needed to start accepting that I would no longer influence decisions at the church. Dr. Sargent had given me room to follow the Lord's directions for my ministry, and I needed to extend Pastor Dailey the same grace. I am confident that Dr. Sargent would not have favored a name change for the church, so I thought I should be just as hands-off toward Pastor Dailey's ministry vision. He moved Bible study from Mondays and Thursdays to Wednesdays and started serving food beforehand. The change went very well, as did serving lunch and dinner before Revive Wednesdays. The lessons he prepared engaged the people, and attendance increased every Wednesday.

In 2019, I took a one-year sabbatical, although I was still in town. While coming around for the construction of The Theater, I purposely avoided contact with the church administration or members. I attended church council meetings twice, but did not participate in any other ministry meetings and offered no opinions regarding the church's direction.

Teaching regarding church doctrine and ministry processes flowed without any intervention from me. Now I had a front row seat to observe just how the church would move even if I were dead. I did not get involved with the church's day-to-day operations, and Pastor Dailey took the church's reins while allowing me to focus on building The Theatre.

As a pastor, I needed to do as much as possible to ensure a smooth transition in leadership. I realized there was only so much I could do, but I did not want to be derelict in my pastoral responsibilities. Pastor Dailey had been with us going on three years, and I know that, being a former pastor, he was growing impatient to take the reins.

My thought process was two-fold: first, to make sure that the church was healthy; and second, to help blend the new pastor and people's relationship. That could only happen in time as the two entities would merge in spirit. I believe that has happened.

Deacon Carter and I had agreed on a date when my retirement would become official—April 1, 2020—and he communicated that date to the church conference. Regardless of where we were in the building process with The Theatre, it would have nothing to do with my retirement.

Chapter Seven
Handing off the Baton

I officially retired April 1, 2020 at age 69. I preached my final sermon as pastor on February 24, 2019, at 10:15 a.m. That was the last time I exerted any authority or preached at the Friendship Community Church. My sermon was taken from the Book of Joshua 1:1, and the following verses, when God announced to Joshua that Moses was dead. Now, Joshua would have to take the leadership baton and lead the people into the Promised Land.

I wanted to communicate to the people of Friendship that after twenty-eight years in this position, it was now time for me to facilitate a smooth transition of leadership. It was time for the leadership of a younger man, Torin T. Dailey, who had been with us for over two years; therefore, he was no stranger.

It was not an accident that Pastor Dailey was with us and served in every pastoral capacity over that time. I felt the people needed an opportunity to get to know him, and he needed to understand the culture at Friendship in my absence. I announced that I would take a yearlong sabbatical. Church members would occasionally see me around, but I would not be involved in the church's day-to-day operations. Again, my focus and goal were to have a seamless transition. Although I felt that I had been preparing Friendship for almost ten years, I knew that God said to me, "Well done!"

I had seen too many instances where new pastors were replacing a long-tenured pastor, and within months one could see the church move into a state of confusion and decline. Maybe some did not see, including Pastor Dailey, but I was working hard to do my part. It was my responsibility to usher in a competent, capable, compassionate, and caring leader.

Having served at Friendship since 1991, I have paid attention to preachers and the length of time they stayed at a church. Although I had seen older pastors in churches all my life, it seemed like many of them would remain in that position as long as breath was in their bodies. I also noticed that the older pastors did not bring the younger pastors' energy, passion, and vision, nor did they attract new members and young adults. It was also apparent that these churches were not fairing as they were during the earlier years of the pastor's tenure. It was easy to identify churches where pastors stayed too long, as they typically were in decline.

In 1986, when I was enrolled at ITC, several of the students traveled to Columbus, Georgia to worship at one of the senior student's home church. The church was about an hour and a half south of the ITC campus. When we arrived, the parking lot was filling up and the sanctuary was packed. The pastor was short in stature and a powerful preacher who elicited the call-and-response style of African-American preaching to perfection. Ushers were positioned around the sanctuary walls, and the choir loft was full. Associate ministers filled the left front center pew. You could sense that this was one of the more progressive churches in the Columbus area. I would estimate five hundred to seven hundred people were in attendance.

In 2015, I traveled back to the same Columbus church to attend the funeral service of a Friendship member's family member. When we entered the sanctuary, above the pulpit was a banner that read "60th Pastor's Anniversary Celebration." From the smell of the building, the ushers' advanced age, and the choir's five members, I sensed a declining church. A once full and vibrant church was now on life support, and the banner above the pulpit affirmed that.

At that moment, the word of the Lord came to me, "Don't tear down what you have built." By those words, I understood that a pastor could stay at a church too long. If he or she cannot see that what once was is no more, the church will die. *"Where there is no vision, the people perish..."* Proverbs 29:18 (KJV).

I had gotten to know Dr. Joseph Roberts relatively well and had watched him navigate his ministry at Ebenezer Baptist Church here in Atlanta, where both Dr. Martin Luther King, Sr. and Jr. had served in pastoral leadership. Dr. Roberts led the church through a massive building project, and shortly after its completion he retired. The church brought in Dr. Raphael Warnock to succeed him.

Dr. Roberts did not leave the Atlanta area, nor did he leave the church. But it was clear that he no longer had his hand on Ebenezer. I admired what Dr. Roberts had done and how he did it. That was my dream for Friendship. Although this approach is not new, more and more churches are embracing this model.

Maybe I was overly cautious because of my succession vision which took almost ten years to roll out and implement. However, I must admit the trust factor was a significant consideration. I embraced firmly the words of the Apostle Paul, "Don't be in a hurry to place your hands on anyone."

Another mentor and friend, Dr. John W Waters, a retired Old Testament professor at ITC and pastor of the Greater Solid Rock Baptist Church in Riverdale, Georgia, taught me a valuable lesson. I watched Dr. Waters retire when I thought he still had possibly three to five more productive and energetic years left to serve. But he told me, "You will know when to retire. When you don't have new ideas, vision is lacking, and energy is low, it is time to retire."

I thought I had done everything possible to prepare Friendship for a leadership change. In turn, the people have been incredibly supportive of my efforts and demonstrated tremendous patience. Following is the final sermon I preached as pastor of Friendship, on February 23, 2020. It was also the day for our annual church conference.

✝✝✝

SERMON
"The Joshua Generation"

Joshua 1:1–3 (NIV): After the death of Moses the servant of the LORD, the Lord said to Joshua son of Nun, Moses' aide: ²"Moses my servant is dead. Now then, you and all these people, get ready to cross the Jordan River into the land I am about to give to them— to the Israelites. ³I will give you every place where you set your foot, as I promised Moses."

As pastor, the time has come for me to communicate with you regarding the future leadership of the Friendship Community Church of College Park, Georgia. I have served Friendship since 1986, and as pastor since 1991. God and I have had conversations about the pastoral leadership transition of our church. God has not surprised me, and I have not surprised you.

In 2011, Mother Ruby Dennis pastor's aide ministry leader (God bless her soul), wanted to have a twentieth pastoral appreciation for me. I thought it to be perfect timing to start preparing you for a transition in leadership. So, we thought it should be called "A Pre-retirement Celebration." I have been praying for and working on this pastoral transition ever since.

I have taken my position as pastor at Friendship very seriously! I have embraced 1 Timothy 5:22 with clarity—to not lay your hand on anyone suddenly. It has been my experience that vacant pulpits have not served churches well, and bad selections have been even worse! We have seen the disruption of churches, splits, fights, heartbreaks, and broken relationships when churches are without a pastor. The Lord placed on my heart some time ago to implement a transitional process whereby the pulpit would not become vacant. Almost four years ago, we started to gauge the interest of persons to serve as my successor. The human resources, deacons, and the church council ministries developed a survey for persons interested in becoming the pastor of the Friendship Community Church.

The group's criterion for potential candidates was:

1. A Master of Divinity degree or terminal degree.
2. A minimum five years of pastoral experience or experience working as a pastor's assistant; and
3. A healthy personal relationship with Jesus Christ.

We received completed surveys from nine pastors (all had preached at Friendship before) from Alabama, Florida, Georgia, Oklahoma, South Carolina, Tennessee, Virginia, and Wisconsin. Once the committee completed the review process, the human resources ministry presented to the church council the name of Torin T. Dailey from Jacksonville, Florida.

The church brought Pastor Dailey on as assistant to the minister. By allowing the potential candidate to serve in the church for a period, the congregation and candidate would have time to get to know one another better. Pastor Dailey has impressed me as a smart, intelligent, and educated man who loves the Lord. He is an excellent student of the Bible, and an outstanding preacher and teacher in my estimation.

I believe that God has ordained Pastor Dailey to be here, but that does not abrogate the responsibility God gave me as pastor. When he and his family first came to Friendship, his wife, Tiffany, and young son, Torin, immediately began to work in the church's ministries. Then Tiffany got pregnant. Now they are rearing two small children, with maybe three or four more on the way.

I have seen so much of Pastor Dailey's commitment to ministry; there is only one crucial aspect that I feel will complete my responsibility as pastor. We have spent over two years getting to know Pastor Dailey and his family. But what we have not seen is Pastor Dailey having sole responsibility for leading the church. That is why I am taking a sabbatical for a year as we continue to finish the Children and Youth Worship and Recreation Center (The Theatre).

You will see me around occasionally during that period, but I will not participate in any church administrative or pastoral decisions. Pastor Dailey will have all the responsibilities of pastor with the title pastor-teacher. I want to apologize to some of you because over the past twelve months I have not been available, in many instances, so that Pastor Dailey could carry out those duties. This experience will be the final observation and engagement for the congregation. Next February, you will confirm or deny Torin T. Dailey as pastor of the Friendship Community Church of College Park, Georgia.

When we first thought of a sabbatical, we envisioned a completed theatre, that I would be in the Holy Land, and I would be writing two books: Building with Your Own Money and A Model for Transitional Leadership. But because of the challenges of building, rain, and trying to save $1.5 million, now during this sabbatical period I will continue to work with others to complete The Theatre. Let me take this opportunity to express praise and thanks to all of you for your service, cooperation, support, faith, and love over the past thirty-three years.

All you know to do is to support the ministries of the Lord's Church. I don't want to call names, but I would be remiss not to mention our leadership, the church council, deacons, trustees, Christian education and Mother Brown, and the mother's ministry. God is faithful, and your devotion to God shows.

There are those of you who sit in the pews and support the ministries of this church. We could not have done our work over the years without you. Over those years, thousands of people have joined the church. Friendship left West Harvard, and now you sit with five structures and over sixty-six acres of land. And God has made us debt-free! To God, be the glory! God showed me years ago that the trouble we encountered was to prepare the way for the one who was to come to focus on ministry and not mess!

Now let me have about twenty minutes or so. In our text, we find the model used for this founder's day and pastoral transition. The leadership transition from Moses to Joshua went without a hitch. After the death of Moses, God called Joshua to lead. From the selected text, we learn and affirm several things about ourselves.

First, Exodus 33:11—The Joshua generation are worshippers. Moses met with God face-to-face, but Joshua did not leave the tent in worship all day. When Moses talked with God, we don't know what that meeting might have been like if the Joshua generation were not in worship. But this we do know—our lives are blessed by God when we worship. Despite what is going on around you, the Joshua generation chooses to worship!

Second, Exodus 17:9—Moses instructs Joshua to choose men and go out and fight. The Joshua generation are fighters. You cannot sit back and expect the devil to give you anything but *hell!* Abraham had to go out and fight for his family and possessions. David had to go out and fight to take back all that God had given. You must fight for your marriage, your children, your community. The Joshua Generation will not just sit back and allow racism on both sides. Self-hatred destroys God's blessings. You must fight!

Now that does not mean you should get a gun or knife; this requires spiritual weaponry. That is why you need the whole armor of God, not Glock or Smith & Wesson. Ephesians 6:11 tells us, "Put on the full armor of God, so that you can take your stand against the devil's schemes."

Third, Numbers 13:16—The Joshua generation is chosen. You are not here by accident; God chose you for this time and space.

When Moses chose spies to go out and survey the land, he first chose Joshua. How can Friendship be in this position if not chosen? How else can we explain a man from Dolomite, Alabama, with no religious training or preacher pedigree coming to Friendship? The closest I came to having a preaching pedigree was a grandfather who sold everything he could get his hands on, and he was a deacon. Or an uncle who took his dog to the church and baptized the dog. Or another uncle who joined the church stoned drunk, got saved, and became the treasurer of the church.

How could people like Friendship—executives, business owners, managers, teachers, administrators, and families—accept one like me as pastor? Please believe me when I tell you, I was chosen and so were you. The Joshua generation is chosen for sure. The Apostle Peter tells us that we are a "chosen generation, a royal priesthood, a holy nation, His own special people, that you may proclaim the praises of Him who called you out of darkness into His marvelous light." (1 Peter 2:9). That means that God can use anyone, anyway, anyhow. Chosen, you are!

Fourth, Joshua 8:30–31—The Joshua generation honors the previous generation. Joshua honored Moses of the last age. He did not lead the people back but advanced them to claim the Land of Promise.

Joshua did not pit the people against Moses, but instead honored him. God said to Joshua, "I will give you what I promised Moses." God showed Moses the Promised Land, but Joshua led the people into that land.

Joshua understood how he got to where he was. A significant problem I see in our community is that we do not honor our history or those who sacrificed their lives to make things better for us. We fail to honor those who came before us by not building upon the foundation they laid.

Engraved on one of the granite benches at the Interdenominational Theological Center's chapel are these words: "A history worth remembering and ancestors worth honoring." All that I have done, all that we have accomplished here at Friendship, would not have happened without Pastors Sargent, Jackson, Lockett, Lovett, Moore, Thomas, Lowe, and other non-pastors.

Don't forget those schools built with nickels and dimes so that we could advance. If you benefited from attending a predominantly White school, don't forget it was our enslaved forbears and HBCUs that got you there. Send money. And if you benefited from elementary school teachers trained through HBCUs, send money! The Black Church is the heart of our community. We cannot tear it down by lending our voices to the world's criticism of the Black Church.

The church is our only out! Just look at where the Lord has brought us from—to this day! Honor those who had nothing, but they helped you. Just look at where we came from and where we are now. Billy Preston had his math all wrong when it comes to God and God's math. Preston said, "Nothing from nothing leaves nothing." But with God, nothing from nothing leaves everything. Remember, it was God who took nothing and built everything. Build upon what God has given. Don't deny your rich history with God and the people God used in your life! The Joshua generation honors the previous generation!

Fifth, Joshua 6:15. The Joshua generation are people of faith. Who in warfare would march around the enemy's wall and expect to be victorious? But by faith in God, the people did as Joshua instructed. On the seventh day, they received a command to shout, and the walls of Jericho came tumbling down. God can do the impossible! The Joshua generation saw their parents, relatives, and friends die in the wilderness because of disobedience. But the Joshua generation continued to advance, believing the promises of God.

When you arrive at the place where you clearly understand that all things are possible with God, then and only then are all things possible for you! The Joshua generation are people of faith!

Sixth, Joshua 1:8. The Joshua generation fully embraced the Word of God. The Joshua generation knows that every Word of God will come to fruition. Regardless of what problems they encountered, this generation knew that they are more than conquers with God.

Peter walked on water by the word of the Lord (Matthew 14:22–33). God said, *"My word will not return void"* (Isaiah 55:11). When God spoke at the creation, and things began to appear, God said, "That's good" (Genesis 1:25).

This generation understands what Jesus said, "Heaven and earth will pass away, but my word will never pass away" (Matthew 24:35). The Joshua generation fully embraces the Word of God!

Seventh, Exodus 3:8. The Joshua generation are people of destiny. Their purpose is to claim what God has promised! God called Moses and told him to go down and deliver Israel out of slavery. "Tell them I will give them a land flowing with milk and honey." That generation wandered in the wilderness for forty years, achieving nothing, and died there.

But the Joshua generation walked right on in and claimed the promise of God because they are people of destiny! They would not be distracted, dislodged, disaffirmed, disconnected, disordered, disjointed, discombobulated, or disbelieving. They moved into their destiny. God has a destination for the Joshua generation. God has a goal, a future for you! Ultimately, we are moving to be with Jesus.

We know that we cannot stay here, so keep moving. Do what the Lord has called you to do here on earth, but ultimately, you want to have a place to live forever! That is the ultimate reality of Jesus going to Calvary. Jesus suffered, bled, and died for our sins, but the good news is that Calvary was not His destination.

Don't give in and don't give up! Keep moving and stay focused and faithful; because I heard Jesus say, *"...when I go and prepare a place for you, I will come again and will take you to myself, that where I am you may be also"* (John 14:3). The Promised Land for the Joshua generation is being in the very presence of God forever! One of these old days, you will move from labor to reward and hear Him say: "Well done, good and faithful servant!" (Matthew 25:23).

People have to understand, and you have to tell them when they are not moving in the right direction, "Baby, I cannot go there. I am going somewhere else!"

When men and women try to trap you for a one-night stand, tell them, "I am sorry, but I am going somewhere."

Let the world know that the God of the universe has promised you a land flowing with milk and honey, and you are on your way to claim it because you are the Joshua generation!

Amen!

Mother Ruby Dennis

Friendship is one of a very few African-American churches where the sanctuary sits on more than sixty-six acres of land with four buildings that offer over 88,000 square feet of ministry space and is debt-free. With all of its land area, facilities, and congregation size, the church would be attractive to many prospective pastors.

In seminary, students would say, "There are two kinds of preachers: those in Atlanta and those trying to get there." There is no doubt that had we put forth a national public search for my successor, the church would have been overwhelmed with applicants, and we were attempting to weed out ungodly motives.

I took to heart what the Lord had communicated to me, so I started planning for my retirement and preparing the church for my departure. I was sixty-one years of age at the time. My goal was not to stay at

Friendship too long, but long enough to implement an effective succession plan to assure a smooth transition. With the assistance of Mother Dennis, we planned the pre-retirement celebration in conjunction with my twentieth year of serving as pastor. We scheduled the worship service for Monday, October 31, and Wednesday, November 2, 2011. The celebration banquet was scheduled for Friday, November 4, 2011. I can never fully express my gratitude for Mother Dennis and her commitment to this process.

Some people were telling me that I was not old enough or too healthy to retire, and that too many good things were going at Friendship. These people were well meaning, but what they did not understand was that I was being guided by the Lord, and I had planned this transition for the good of both the church and pastor. This was the announcement for my pre-retirement, and at the time I had no idea when I would retire. I depended on God for that date.

I had not taken removing myself from leadership lightly. It was vital for me to continue to be a good steward of where the Lord had allowed me to serve. Friendship is not my church but the Lord's, and the Lord has done miraculous things there. And I am convinced that we have yet to see the tremendous power of God in that church.

The words of the Apostle Paul arrested me when he wrote to Timothy, *"Do not be hasty in the laying on of hands...,"* (1 Timothy 5:22).

Although the Lord had led me to the point of this decision, I had not strategized how to go about identifying the person who might succeed me. In the two years following my pre-retirement, I invited a broad spectrum of preachers to come in and preach special days, one-night revivals, and teach. None of them knew that they would be interviewing for the position, nor did I tell any of the leaders what was on my mind.

I called together the human resources coordinator, the deacon's leader, and the trustee leader, and we met and gave the church council names of persons we may want to consider. Each of them had been to the church more than once. The council had heard them preach and teach.

Yvette Hart (human resources), Deacon Henry Carter (deacons' leader), and Johnny Mitchell (trustees' leader), worked together to devise a plan to identify my successor. I provided the names of nine ministers they were familiar with. We generated a survey to be completed by all interested persons.

We did not make a public announcement of the impending opening because God led me not to open this position; I was totally against a vacant pulpit announcement. The goal was to identify someone and have that person hired on staff and spend time with the church and its ministries.

I contacted each person to gauge his level of interest, and all of them were interested. One of the criteria was that the persons we considered was already serving as a pastor or had worked closely with a pastor. The requirements included the minimum of a Master of Divinity degree, pastoral experience to lead and manage more than 3,000 congregants and nearly one hundred ministries with multiple buildings. When we received the completed surveys and their qualifications and biographical material, we all met, and based upon our personal experience with the candidates, discussed each one's merits. When the study ended, the group began a process of elimination.

I was determined not to weigh in, but I did have a preference. I wanted to stay clear of the perception that I was putting this person in the position. I had seen from a distance where churches used that excuse not to embrace the new pastor, thus causing longterm problems.

They came up with a name among the group of prospects, but that was not the end of the process. They asked me what I thought of their selection based upon the requirements we had put forth. I told them that I trusted their judgment and I was willing to go along with their recommendation.

The selection process required the group to include their rationale. The church council knew all the candidates, and they agreed with the proposal. The Lord blessed us again.

It appeared the process used for a seamless transition was well on its way without me having input. All the candidates possessed the qualifications as put forth by the group.

When the church council agreed that we should reach out to Torin T. Dailey, I called him and told him of the council's decision. I had spent some time with all the candidates, and I had learned from Pastor Dailey's wife that they had an interest in moving to Atlanta because she had lived in here previously and was familiar with the city.

That was important to me because I had given thought to family separation, even if only for a short time, when I was being considered for a church in Columbus, Georgia, as well as one in Meridian, Mississippi. Pastor Dailey told me that he was still interested, but that he had to pray about it and have conversations with his family and church. When he followed up with me, I asked human resources to get involved and work out his transition from Jacksonville, Florida.

He and his family joined in with the Friendship family as if they had been there all the time. He was very respectful of the church and of me, and Mrs. Dailey immediately began supporting the church's ministries, and their son Torin joined the children's choir and Cub Scouts.

When Pastor Dailey came, I wanted the church to distinguish between the two of us. When I received my Doctor of Ministry from United Theological Seminary in Dayton, Ohio, in 2007, I asked the church not to refer to me as "Doctor Bryant," as I had always been "Pastor Bryant."

But when Pastor Dailey came, I instructed the office staff to use the title Doctor on all communications pertaining to me. I was then referred to as Dr. Bryant, and Torin Dailey was Pastor Dailey, who came on board with the title assistant to the pastor. After a year, his title changed to assistant pastor. This title change was also done in part so that the title Pastor Dailey would flow into his eventual title and role.

Although my retirement and Pastor Dailey's installation took a little longer than we both anticipated, there were some loose ends I had to tighten up for myself, for Pastor Dailey, and for the church. The Lord gave us the luxury of time, and we were able to move the church forward so that my family's care and I would not be a burden on his ministry.

Dr. E. Dewey Smith of the House of Hope is a friend who has preached at Friendship on several occasions. Once, when I was visiting his church, I told him how much I appreciated the way he honored the former pastor,

S. L. Shepherd. Pastor Shepherd's widow is still among them, and Dr. Smith and the church have continued to support her even though Pastor Shepherd has been deceased for several years.

I had observed how the House of Hope had spent millions to upgrade and maintain its facility, yet there was still a budget line item to support Mrs. Shepherd. Dr. Smith had not neglected his predecessor in order to address his own ministry agenda.

After a year and a half, I could see Pastor Dailey's anxiousness growing. He was ready to take the mantle of leadership at Friendship. But some things needed to take place before the full transition could occur. One of the things I wanted to ensure was that his Friendship compensation was slightly higher after he and his family left Jacksonville. It was important that by coming to Friendship, he and his family's lifestyle did not suffer.

What was most impressive to me about Pastor Dailey was that I witnessed firsthand how patience became a virtue he could claim. He was ready to take Friendship to another level, still he remained patient until the time was right. Over this period, I also noticed the amount of time he put into study and his teaching and preaching commitment. We often would bump into each other at hospitals and hospice facilities. Although he was relatively young, I could see that he had a pastor's heart.

Years ago, when our church was going through court battles, the Lord had given me peace and I embraced the trials before me. The Lord blessed me to know that I was going through that experience so that my successor would not have to go through the same thing, but instead could focus on ministry. And that is what I have seen in Pastor Dailey over these years.

Pastor Dailey and I had only one tense moment during the transition process, and he handled it like a mature Christian. When it appeared that the offer given to him was missing something, he and the human resources ministry met a couple of times. I did suggest to him, "Whatever they offer you, take it." I knew the people, and I knew whatever they offered would be acceptable and above the area's average pastor's package.

Almost a year earlier, Torin had told me that they were building a new home. With that in mind, we spoke one day, and I told him that I had a house where he and his family could live. I remembered that when Friendship was voting on my tenure multiple times, one member said to me, "And they don't care about your family. Where will you live?"

Although I knew the church council and human resources members, I also knew how people can change. So, my comments were to give comfort and support; in other words, what I was trying to convey that if he and the church could not come to terms, he would not have to be concerned about his family's living conditions.

And that is when the wisdom of Torin blessed me, and that sealed my faith in him. His response to what I said was, "Dr. Bryant, I have learned that there are times when I should say nothing. You have a good evening." What I said to him had not gone over as intended.

Torin's words caused me to grow because I am known to have, if not the last word, the one next to it. I guess I needed to take some of my advice. I have told couples and others regarding conflict that, "no one is getting a trophy" for winning an argument. Therefore, "winning" is not productive, but rather, reconciliation is the goal. Early in my marriage, my wife taught me that I could not argue by myself. Pastor Dailey had done several things to make me think that he would be suitable for Friendship, but nothing he ever said or did ever had such a profound impact on me as the words he said that day.

We set the retirement banquet for me for March 13, 2020, and the retirement worship service on Sunday, March 15, 2020, at 10:15 a.m. The banquet was fabulous and authentic to my temperament. There was no head table; I wanted to be among the people. We thoroughly enjoyed reflections, entertainment, food, and mingling with the people. According to the planners, there were over seven hundred people in attendance. During the time we were in the banquet hall, I visited every table.

On Sunday, the New Bethlehem Baptist Church of Dolomite's, pastor, Joseph Edwards, preached a powerful and effective sermon, and he blessed the church. After the services, the church prepared a beautiful reception in the family life center and the J. H. Lockett Fellowship Hall. Indeed it was a day to remember.

We had determined that the church was not meeting for worship on March 22, 2020, because of COVID-19 restrictions; however, we followed through with a scheduled church council meeting. We had set the installation service for Pastor Dailey for Sunday, March 22, at the 10:15 a.m. service. We held the scheduled church council meeting on Tuesday, March 17, at 7:00 p.m., but we did not know when we would resume a regular worship service. I asked the church council to install Pastor Dailey that evening.

Once explained, the church council was in full support of the idea, and we moved forward with installing Torin T. Dailey as pastor. But I sensed some reservations with Pastor Dailey. I believe he felt that the installation service would not have been authentic unless scheduled and carried out in the sanctuary with all the people present.

But I was unsure how long churches would be mandated to refrain from gathering to slow the coronavirus spread. This way, regardless of what the state would decide, the church had installed its new pastor. I assured Pastor Dailey that he could schedule the installation service as he pleased whenever it was right. He and I had agreed that I would do both charges to the pastor and the church.

The church council had been given authority by the church to act on its behalf. Had we waited until the state lifted those restrictions, only God knows how long that would have been. If the council acted, the church would embrace the installation because on the fourth Sunday of February during an official church conference, two hundred and eighty-two members were present. All who were present that night had affirmed Torin T. Dailey as the new pastor of the Friendship Community Church, effective immediately after my retirement on April 1, 2020.

The church had never held a worship service online, but Pastor Dailey did an excellent job implementing streaming services by Sunday, March 22, 2020. Friendship did not miss a beat in streaming worship services and Bible studies.

The government offered a Payroll Protection Plan (PPP), and Pastor Dailey was interested in applying for it. I have always had concerns about government and church engaging in financial arrangements. Pastor Dailey explained to me, "As pastor emeritus with the responsibility of leader of the corporation, you would have to sign documents for the PPP."

It reminded me of how God provided when banks would not loan us money because of the letters sent out by the opposition when we were trying to build. I had seen how God provided for us in every situation, and even now we were not hurting for finances; we were debt-free. I passionately believed that we did not need to run to the government, and I compared it to Israel wanting to go back to Egypt once freed. I explained that God had provided for us in the past, and God would continue to do so. We did not need to go to the government for any assistance and become enslaved to them. Some churches may have benefited from this program, but I felt that Friendship did not need to be among them.

I did not want to get in the way of what God was showing Pastor Dailey, so after explaining my position, I said, "You are the pastor." But I also told him that I would not be willing to sign anything if my assets or I were a guarantor tied to any government obligations. I have never known the government to be entirely fair. And I did not believe that the government was giving away anything for nothing. Therefore, I thought it best for us to continue to trust God. But if God was leading him to do this, with those exceptions, I would do it.

Friendship has not met as a congregation since March 2020 because of the coronavirus pandemic. The governor opened the state for worship services, still, Pastor Dailey was not willing to hold services until he knew the congregation would be safe. Statistics show that African Americans are dying of COVID-19 at rates that are disproportionate to Whites. I am convinced that Pastor Dailey will prayerfully do what is best for his flock.

Conclusion

Through It All

At the heart of my young adult life and ministerial experience is faith in God. When I was growing up, I was not conscious of faith's significance in understanding my relationship with God. More important, I did not realize that my life could not and would not be complete without God. While focused on the external, it was the internal that made all the difference in my life. My parents did not talk about faith per se around our house, but later in my life, I was able to see how they demonstrated faith in God every day.

Our community and my family's faith in God led to our deliverance even in such a racist and oppressive environment. It was due to my faith in God that my life was turned around at age 33, in Dolomite, Alabama. And my journey from mimicking the preacher at Tuskegee University to leading the Friendship Community Church of College Park, Georgia, as pastor was simply a miraculous move of God.

I still am amazed to hear people talk about the great job we did at Friendship during all the turmoil, or should I say our testing. Over those ten years, everywhere I went—inside or outside of the state—when people learned who I was, they would say, "I am praying for you." But when the dust settled, and people could see what God had done through us by keeping our church together and completing the building project, they said, "It is a miracle what God has done!"

I wrote this book, *I Didn't Want to Do It*, first because it is true. As you have read and seen, becoming a church pastor was not on my radar. Second, I needed to show others what God can do when one might think that he or she is ill-equipped to do extraordinary things for God.

What is most amazing to me is that quitting never entered my thinking despite all the opposition's tactics and attacks toward me. Sometimes I reflect on the movie The Blues Brothers about the musicians who were on a mission from God. Although they encountered various obstacles, nothing diminished their focus. They were on a mission from God.

After experiencing the vision God revealed to me, I was on a mission from God, and I was determined to do my part to bring that vision to pass. I would recommend that anyone who wants to get on the right side of God and move a ministry forward first repent and then turn to God. I have learned that when you fully trust and depend on God, miracles happen, and everything God has said will come to pass. I also believe that we are "workers together" with God! If God has given you a vision, you must do your part, and God will produce everything you need.

When our church was going through all the disruptions, I never lost faith in God. I never thought that anything the opposition did or said or that entered their minds caught God by surprise. I am convinced that God knew their thoughts even before those thoughts were entertained. God knew their actions before they even took one step. God's preparation for what was to come was unmatched by anything I could see.

I have come to understand firsthand that my experience in the church is not unique. It happens all the time. And to everyone on the Lord's side, the enemy will come; but remember, God will never leave. The antichrist works through people to hinder and halt God's work. God takes those experiences to test and prepare the believer for anything that might come his or her way.

God is faithful! The psalmist said it best, *"Wait on the LORD; Be of good courage, And He shall strengthen your heart; Wait, I say, on the Lord!"* (Psalm 27:14).

It took almost thirty-five years for me to begin to understand the power of God operating in the lives of people. Looking back at my life and knowing firsthand of what God was dealing with in me, it is just amazing to see how the Lord used me to move a people from a small church on the corner to build a new campus with more than sixty-six acres of land and over 88,000 square feet of ministry space. But more critical, thousands of people united with the church from every walk of life.

I am amazed at how God intervened in my life and did something that I could never have imagined. My outlook on life as a youth and a young adult never included a ministerial career, not to mention being involved in God's miraculous move in developing people and constructing a church campus. I could never have imagined that I could lead a church in reaching people to accept Jesus Christ as Lord and Savior and lead a congregation in erecting a multi-million-dollar ministry complex.

That said, I never expected to encounter people in the church who were willing to do anything to stop God's work, even to the point that they would go to court and obtain a restraining order to keep me out of the pulpit and without any spiritual, legal, or moral basis to do so. But God is good! God gave me the gift of faith and perseverance, along with the assurance of God's presence so that I could participate in a remarkable ministry, regardless of the enemy's attacks.

No matter what your career path or your station in life, a partnership with God can make all things possible for you. I have heard some people say, "I don't get involved in religion; I am spiritual." I want to encourage all of those who are spiritual and others to establish a personal relationship with Jesus, the Christ. In so doing you will see how God works through Him in you to accomplish impossible things in your life.

After experiencing the vision God revealed to me, I was on a mission from God, and I was determined to do my part to bring that vision to the pass. Since that night in Dolomite, when I repented and decided to turn from people who had not been beneficial for my life and seek the cause of Christ, my life has never been the same.

I never thought that I would lead a congregation and, for sure, never felt that we could build a church campus without burdening the people

Pastor Bryant leading a ceremony with two Friendship members

with a lifetime of debt. What God did was utterly unique, and to God, I give the praise. Building this campus debt-free first required a vision from God; second, fully embracing that vision; and third, acting on that vision and celebrating God as the pieces were coming together. I used to hear people in the church sing, "He may not come when you want Him, but He'll be there right on time!" After a failed attempt to secure a bank loan, I was determined to depend on God. It took time for the project to come together, but like everything else, the Lord gave us all that we needed— including time.

Although the Bible clearly states it, I would like people to know that "All things are possible with God." If you have God on your side, nothing, nothing, nothing will be impossible for you!

When I reflect on this marvelous life experience, God allows me to share something Deacon Howard Green, Sr., told me, "God will provide for you everything you need."

A Look in Pictures
A Blessed Life

Rachel, Brenda, and Donald Bryant

Rachel smiling with Daddy

Rachel Michelle Bryant graduating from Alabama State University

Pastor Bryant with Congressman John Lewis

Tennis and basketball courts at Friendship Community Church

**Pastor Bryant with
Dr. Joseph Lowery**

**Pastor Bryant with
Pastor Willie Bolden**

Pastor E. Dewy Smith and Pastor George Smith with Pastor Bryant

The Bryants with Secretary of State Hillary Clinton

Pastor Bryant horseback riding at a church fellowship

About the Author
Donald Earl Bryant, DMin

D r. Donald Earl Bryant is pastor emeritus at the Friendship Community Church of College Park, Georgia. He is founder, CEO, and president of DEB Ministries, Inc., a community development corporation that establishes scholarships and 529 college saving funds for children and youth. The ministry supports other non-profit organizations in community initiatives.

The Alabama native earned a Bachelor of Science degree from Tuskegee University, a Master of Divinity (MDiv) from the Interdenominational Theological Center in Atlanta, and a Doctor of Ministry degree from United Theological Seminary in Dayton, Ohio.

Dr. Bryant is married to the former Brenda Lea Williams, and they have two adult children.